From Pain to Purpose

A complete guide for healing PTSD

Applying Holographic theory in reversing the effects of Post-Traumatic Stress Disorder, anxiety, and emotional pain.

Dr Gabe Roberts, DC, Msc.D

Editor: Tiffany Roberts
Front and back cover design: Tiffany Roberts

A special gift for you, reader:

Grab your free course on the subconscious mind.

FROM PAIN TO PURPOSE
COURSE

https://thesubconscioushealer.com/frompaintopurposebook

MOTIVATE AND INSPIRE OTHERS!
"Share this book"
Retail price $24.99

Special Quantity Discount

5-20 books	20.99 each
21-99 books	17.99 each
100-499 books	10.95 each
500-999 books	8.95 each
1000+ Books	6.95 each

To place an order contact:
elevateyourfield@pm.me

Dedication

I dedicate this to my wife, Tiffany and to my children because you have shown me a brighter side of life that made me want to get better. If you weren't in my life, I wouldn't have gotten out of rock bottom.

Forward

In the journey of life, we often encounter moments of profound challenge, experiences that imprint themselves deeply within our being, shaping the lens through which we perceive the world. For some, these encounters manifest as traumatic events, leaving scars that extend far beyond the physical realm, affecting the very core of who we are.

Post-Traumatic Stress Disorder (PTSD) and its accompanying companions—anxiety, emotional pain, and the myriad of symptoms they entail—can seem insurmountable, casting shadows that obscure the path to healing and purpose.

In "From Pain to Purpose: A Complete Guide for Healing PTSD," Dr. Gabe Roberts invites us on a transformative journey, one that transcends the conventional boundaries of healing. Drawing upon the profound insights of holographic theory, Dr. Roberts unveils a groundbreaking approach to reversing the effects of trauma, illuminating the path from suffering to profound purpose.

Within the pages of this book, Dr. Roberts masterfully guides us through the intricate web of our consciousness, revealing the profound interconnectedness between mind, body, and spirit.

With clarity and compassion, he elucidates the holographic nature of our being, where every experience, every emotion, is encoded within the very fabric of our existence. Yet, in his wisdom, Dr. Roberts shows us that we need not unravel the intricacies of each trauma; instead, he offers us the key to accessing fragments of our holographic data, empowering us to effect profound change from within.

As we journey through the chapters of this transformative guide, Dr. Roberts equips us with the tools and techniques necessary for deep healing to occur. From the foundational importance of hydration to the intricate mechanisms of trauma, each page is imbued with wisdom, offering practical insights that transcend the confines of traditional therapy.

Through the lens of holographic deletion and or holographic reframing, Dr. Roberts unveils a pathway to liberation, guiding us to clear the imprints of past traumas and reclaim our innate wholeness.

Yet, beyond the realm of individual healing, "From Pain to Purpose" offers us a profound insight into the very essence of human existence.

Dr. Roberts reminds us that we are not merely physical beings bound by the constraints of time and space; rather, we are luminous beings, radiant with the potential for growth, transformation, and boundless love.

Through the lens of love and forgiveness, he invites us to transcend the limitations of our past, embracing a future filled with possibility and purpose.

In the words of Dr. Roberts, "The power is within you. Are you ready?" As we embark upon this journey of self-discovery and healing, may we heed his call, embracing the profound truth that the only way for change to manifest in our lives is for us to change ourselves.

With "From Pain to Purpose" as our guide, may we unlock the latent potential within, embracing a future imbued with joy, abundance, and profound purpose.

Dr. Gabe Roberts has gifted us with a roadmap to liberation, illuminating the path from pain to purpose. May we walk this path with courage, compassion, and an unwavering commitment to healing.

Buy this book, read it, apply it, and share it. Our wonderful world needs all the health that it can get!!!

Robert A Rakowski, DC, CCN, DACBN, DIBAK; Clinic Director, The Natural Medicine Center, Houston, TX.

A Note from The Author

Congratulations on your endeavor that has led to you having this book in your hand, as this book will give you more than you might think.

You will learn specific causes for nearly all sources of panic attacks, the mechanisms behind Post Traumatic Stress Disorder, nervousness, and anxiety as well as the significant contributing factors that lead to the development of most chronic illnesses. You will also be given the answer to why people suffer from these types of mental challenges and easy practical solutions to completely reverse it.

This book is for people who want to achieve more out of themselves as well as those who are feeling as though they have lost a significant part of their health. You will finish this book with a clear picture of how your mind and body work together and be able to look at yourself as well as other people and know how to figure out complex things that may have been opposing you for years on why people do the things they do and why change is so difficult.

Many of these ideas are not ours originally, as I have numerous mentors and studied everything from Soviet sport psychology, hypnosis, to the Gateway Process (a de-classified CIA report on the brain), consciousness, and holographic coding of how memories and thought processes work.

Many of these are what led us to developing Holographic Manipulation Therapy®, a technology for generating deep and powerful changes that this book will introduce you into experiencing. Through years of study and clinical practice, in thousands of patients as well as ourselves, we have put them together in an easy-to-follow very user-friendly format to simplify the best approach to changing the things about you that perhaps you don't like or are holding you back.

After all, the only way for things to change in your life, _is for you to change_. That is the truth and along with that comes another truth that we must acknowledge. Change is uncomfortable.

Sometimes we have the desire to change but are not certain of the way to begin it. Let this book act as a guide on helping you take the first steps forward into change. People start by getting smart on the subject of changing themselves, and study.

They go over affirmations. They journal. They put up vision boards of who they want to be and how they would like to live, yet still have "something" in their way.

This is an unforeseen barrier that is preventing any progress. This book is proposed for those who want to change yet run into these invisible barriers. Following the instructions and understanding the knowledge presented in this book will give you an exact science for the removal of these invisible barriers and allow you to witness explicit changes in all areas of your life. Study it. Stick with it. Believe me, there is nothing simpler for removing these walls and unconscious limitation then what will be presented to you.

Repeat the process and as you begin to feel different, as you notice the barriers crumbling away, you will witness changes in your life that you've never imagined. I certainly have and so have others who have followed these teachings and took them seriously.

Some authorities may try to discount what is given here.

To anyone who tries I will confidently say this: let's line up 200 people who are stricken with panic disorders, PTSD, anxiety, depression, digestive disturbances, and other chronic conditions. Of these 200 people, the skeptical ones can take 100 and I will take 100. We will both implement our best techniques (and soon you will become competent in them from reading, understanding and applying what you learn from this book) And when the dust finally clears, and we have taken both groups of our people as far as we can, in the direction of feeling peace, calm and obtaining deep harmony within themselves, the resulting scores will let everyone know exactly what works and what doesn't.

Please understand this--I am not looking for challenges. I am only making the point that we must *start promoting what works* and not what strokes the coat of institutions such as high-tech medical science in mainstream education.

Amongst my research are the detailed accounts of over 300 near death experiences that are documented from people who had actually felt themselves leave their body yet were able to come back into the physical form returning to their body but arriving with a new perspective.

Additionally, I have interviewed over half a dozen people who have experienced it firsthand. The similarities that these people generally have and share during this phenomenon is nothing short of eye opening.

They all agree that there is a complete state of bliss unlike anything they've ever experienced as well as a deep sensation of being accepted, without a grain of any burdens and simultaneously being aware that they are, suddenly, everywhere at once. They were complete energy without mass. It profoundly moved them and gives them an experience that sometimes may be even difficult to put into words. But I think the most appropriate explanation for this is that we all return to a state of pure consciousness when we die.

As Wayne Dyer says there's a part of us that was never born and will never die.

That part is consciousness. As we go through this book, you'll see some striking evidence of how this consciousness is an invisible link between everyone and everything.

The state of bliss, love, and acceptance that people experience can best be summarized in five words: *We become one with Divine.* If this is what happens when we leave the physical body, we returned to consciousness and become one with our Divine Creator, what happens before we're born?

The answer is simple: we start out this way. Before we are in physical form, we are pure consciousness, and we remain pure consciousness our entire existence although we lose this awareness and perception and we lose it in a very profound way. And most of the time, we lose this during our time in the womb.

We start out as pure consciousness, light, love, infinite and only knowing the presence of God and then through the process of conception we go from ethereal to physical form into a single cell.

Now this connection with God is still very present with us and it's all we know until the moment we come in contact with our *first outside suggestion from the world*. In this book, we will talk about childhood trauma and its devastating effects, but before our childhood even begins, we are often times already set up for disaster.

How? Because before we were ever born in many cases, we have already "lost" that connection with God.

During the moment of conception is when we are the most absorbent in acquiring information from our environment. Like metal filings being drawn to a magnet or water is drawn to a dry sponge, we are absorbing tremendous amounts of information from the environment. For each passing hour after conception, we become less and less and less absorbent. A sponge absorbs the most water when it's the driest and this is when we are the absolute driest. At this point, we are equivalent to a blank hard drive with the capacity to store tremendous amounts of information yet have no data. This is the critical time in our life when we are the most vulnerable because we have no data, we have nothing to compare or judge any past experience against.

At this point we are still connected with God until we encounter something referred to as an Initial Synthesizing Event, or ISE as we will call it.

The ISE is the moment that changes everything.

The initial sensitizing event is when we first become separated from God by learning our first human experience. Once we have our first human experience- like a dry sponge getting a single drop of water- it quickly absorbs every bit of the data and instantly becomes a perception.

That first perception can be compared to an egg being cracked and poured onto a skillet. Imagine what an egg looks like on a skillet with a yolk and the surrounding white.

 This is the very beginning of what becomes our subconscious mind.

What is the point of this? Because whatever is interfering with you trusting the process of life, loving yourself to the fullest or holding you back is something you learned.

Before we start, I want to point out that when you were conceived, you were perfect.

You could say you were even born as a perfect image of Divine light. Have you ever wondered why you're attracted to a newborn baby?

It doesn't matter the race, skin color, the religion. If you ever notice a random stranger who is a mother or father standing in front of you in the shopping line at the grocery store, you'll notice a strong urge to reach out and touch their baby. You may notice a deep urge to want to hold it, even though you don't know the people. You'll look hesitantly at the parent just so you can touch the little baby's hand and let it hold onto your finger.

Why do you think that is? What is causing such a strong magnetic pull towards a newborn baby?

Why? Because they are fresh from God. Pure.

You see, we are created in a magnificent vibration of pure light. It is our conditioning that takes place after birth where our problems arise from.

You can change it. It takes ruthless determination, guts, and *making the decision* to change it, no matter what.

Following what this book tells you will absolutely change your life. Throughout the years, we've had various doctors, chiropractors, lawyers, psychiatrists, and some of the most senior executives from various companies tell us there's nothing that equals these teachings. Why? Because we're giving you an understanding to a person of *who they really are.*

This book is not just giving them some technique or intellectual understanding or physical or academic lesson. That would do virtually no good. It is the power within you that makes the difference.

The power is within you.

Are you ready?

Let's start from the beginning.

CHAPTER 1

My Childhood Prepared me for this work.

"As traumatized children, we always dreamed that someone would come and save us. We never dreamed that it would, in fact, be ourselves as adults." – Alice Little

In 1979 I was born in Wagner, Oklahoma and grew up with a mother and my older brother as well as two younger twin siblings. From the earliest years I can remember, every one of my childhood memories was saturated with agony, pain, misery, neglect, emotional and physical abuse with days of just not wanting to be alive. Most of my alone times were spent hoping for an escape from this ongoing cycle of sheer mayhem.

I don't recall any days of my childhood where I had ever laughed or smiled or just had an enjoyable experience.

The reason is that I was born into an abusive household where alcohol abuse was regular thing and along with it, came violent and physical abuse from my stepfather.

I never knew my biological father growing up because my mother and father divorced long before I was the age to be aware of these kinds of things.

Looking back throughout my entire life I spent very little time with my biological father. I could count on one hand how many times I spent any time with him and so I knew very little about him, other than a few stories about how severe his alcoholism was.

In fact, my mother once told me that the very day she went into labor with me was one that can be described as pure havoc. My uncle had to forcibly entered our house and desperately attempt to get my father to wake up because he was so drunk, he was passed out and laying on the floor. He was literally yelling at my father's limp body, "Hey wake up! Your wife's going into labor!"

So, as I later discuss the details about how the early experiences shape our brain, form our personality, and the baseline status of our nervous system, this was the start of my first day being born onto earth. It was also laying down the foundations of my own journey with Post Traumatic Stress Disorder--- a syndrome that I would come to know intimately.

Most of my childhood before the age 10 was living with my mother, who was battling her own traumas, and as such, was emotionally unavailable to both me and my older brother. Coloring this picture was also a very violent, toxic relationship with my stepfather, who had hos own unresolved wounds and was a severe alcoholic.

You may notice this pattern of alcoholism emerging from partners my mother chose. It is important to point out that this is not necessarily unique. As a rule, when it comes to relationships, people will tend to seek out a partner based on similar levels of passed experienced unresolved trauma. The reason will become more apparent later.

Behavioral patterns repeat themselves at unconscious levels and these are unintentional tendencies and drivers that cause a person to choose a specific type of partner. It is based on finding similar characteristics, patterns or what gives them certain feelings that match an internal checklist of what they are seeking out based on *what's familiar*.

In other words, people will look for a partner who gives them similar feelings to what they themselves had experienced between the years of zero to five years old.

In my mother's example, she had a very destructive marriage with a severe alcoholic who was extremely violent, and, in some way, she was mimicking the feelings that reflect dynamics of her own childhood. We all do this without knowing it.

If you look at the cases of battered wife syndrome, the question most often asked when people hear of a woman who has been repeatedly abused or beaten by her partner is, "Why does she stay with him?" Or let's say the family of the woman steps in and helps the woman relocate away from the abusive partner only to find a short time later that she went back to him and now the questions is: "Why on earth would she go back to him?"

It is because it was not a conscious choice or decision made by her intellectual mind. It was an unconscious driver to seek out what *felt* familiar and when this woman was beginning a new life away from this man, it was an unfamiliar feeling. It is this unfamiliar feeling that grows and becomes so uncomfortable to her, it eventually proliferates enough to cause her to move right back in with her abusive partner, even if the circumstances were potentially life threatening.

We will later cover the details of the unconscious, or subconscious, mind and compare it to the conscious mind so you have a better understanding of how they work, and this example will make more sense.

My older brother and I did not see a day go by when we weren't desperately wanting to escape the wrath of our drunken stepfather. We could be spending hours playing with GI Joe figures on the floor of our house, using our imagination to escape the environment, even if it was temporary. I can recall one moment when my stepdad was not paying attention as he walked by and stepped on one of our plastic GI Joe accessories. The toy hurt his foot so much he let out a groan and instantly went into a rage, yanking off his belt and began hitting us with it. This kind of disability to regulate his own emotions gives a glimpse of his own wounds.

Young children have no ability to manage or adjust their own emotions, so they are completely dependent on the healthy emotional management of a parent or adult to regulate their own emotions. If the adult, in this situation being my stepfather, never had the right environmental surroundings during his infancy or childhood to learn how to manage his emotions, then he never himself develops that ability. The result is an immature adult unable to self-regulate their emotional state, leading to a sudden burst of rage, belt in hand.

Whatever was in the way of this swinging belt was getting struck--it didn't matter whether it was our bottoms, our head, our back, or our hands. There were times when we could not walk for a few days after some of these beatings he gave us.

This happened so frequently that it was a way of life for us. One time he did it with such a fury to us that my older brother defecated himself right in the middle of getting beaten.

The years of my earliest youth were just saturated with fear of this man. Fear of his yelling, fear of him beating us, fear of him being intoxicated and verbally calling us fools, and fear of watching him violently get into physical altercations with my mom.

In fact, I remember watching him physically throw her completely out of the front door when he was highly intoxicated and after a long-drawn-out argument.

All these situations, including living in constant fear and being surrounded by violence, occurred before I was six years old, the most crucial time for a developing child's brain and self-image. The brain's center for controlling stress throughout our life, referred to as the HPA axis, describing the neurological pathways between the hypothalamus, pituitary gland and the adrenal glands are structured during these years, including time in the womb until around age five. Stress, overwhelming moments from violence or abuse during this critical developmental period can distort how our body perceives and responds to stress throughout our lifetime.

Between the years of zero to three years old, our brain develops at the most rapid rate throughout our entire lives. During these times our neurological processes are connecting so quickly that there are approximately one million synaptic connections per second.

Most, but certainly not all of our brain development occurs after birth and outside of the womb. By the end of the third year of life, our human brain is roughly 80% the size of an adults, however our human body is roughly 19% the size of an adult.

Moreover, all this brain development is under the direct impact of environmental influences. From the respected Journal in Pediatrics, the Harvard Center on the Developing Child published February of 2012 states that there is growing scientific evidence demonstrates that social and physical environments that threaten human development because of scarcity, stress or stability can lead to short term physiologic and psychological adjustments that are necessary for immediate survival and adaptation which may come with a significant cost to long term outcomes in learning, behavior, health and longevity.

In other words, the adaptations that my older brother and I were forced to resort to, in response to such a threatening environment, perhaps helped us endure the early difficulties but these same adaptations also invertedly become sources of pathology later in life and are known to even shorten longevity.

In my later teenage and adult life, it was Post Traumatic Stress Disorder (PTSD) amongst several others. For my brother, he has experienced chronic symptoms of psoriasis on his skin.

PTSD is associated with an underlying emotional condition of not trusting the process of life, fear of life, anger and/or guilt from an overwhelming experience. Psoriasis, being visible on the skin, a sensory organ, is associated with fear of being hurt and can originate from a deadening of the senses related to the self. [2]

We will cover more detail of this, including the mechanisms, how the body responds and how to resolve these kinds of challenges in later chapters. It is important to realize the role from our early environmental experiences, you can see how whatever happens emotionally to us in the developmental stages of life, will often manifest later in our adult life.

When most of your brain develops inside an environment filled with these kinds of conditions, your nervous system becomes wired in specific ways, and you begin to view the world as a potential threat because of the circuitry responsible for scanning and evaluating potential threats is altered to function on repetitive cycles of high alert.

There were other parts of my childhood that was less threatening, but no less damaging. Today, as a Chiropractor specializing in Psychosomatic Medicine, these underlying patterns are collectively the most common factor I witness clinically in my patients who suffer chronic conditions.

The psychologist Dr Gordon Neufeld uses the word *attachment* as a necessity for closeness in both physical and emotional proper development. It is an indispensable requirement when we come into this world. Attachment and connection are biological necessities for health, just as clean drinking water and good nutrition are. My mother not only allowed my stepfather to treat her children this way without stepping in to protect us but was highly emotionally unavailable herself.

My older brother and I felt isolated from any kind of emotional nourishment, although we did in some respects have each other, our mother was all too busy focusing on other things, including her new relationship after she finally divorced my stepfather after numerous occurrences of physical abuse, verbal and emotional abuse and constant infidelity.

Although it was a significant relief when we was no longer in our home, things did not get much better.

There was no attention, emotional acceptance, and very little comfort from her. I can recall one instance when my older brother and I were very hungry, and she made us a PB&J sandwich. She then sent us both to bed when it was still very early in the day, with plenty of daylight out.

Her new boyfriend, who happened to be the cousin of her newly divorced husband, came over to our house. As my older brother and I were in our room, given harsh instructions to not come out, we could smell the aroma and hear the sounds of fresh fish being fried, as she was in the process of making him a gourmet meal.

This points out another important cause of trauma. Trauma can occur in an infant or child when good things were supposed to happen yet *did not*. There are multiple ways that trauma wounds a child, but this one in particular occurs when emotional requirements not being met during vital moments or the experiences of not being seen, heard, felt or accepted. Summarized by Dr Bessel Van Der Kolk: Trauma is when we are not seen and not known; it represents a fracturing of one's self by a core need not being fulfilled.

It was obvious, looking back that she was battling her own internal wounds, and sometimes they were expressed as moments of amplified anger. It was not just my stepfather who struck us, as she would regularly hit my brother and myself when she was furious about something often using that same paddle that my he did. It was a dreadful piece of wood, carved from a 2x4 into an oar shaped board that was used more times on us then I can remember.

Sometimes moments of my childhood trauma were expressed with neglect, as in the case I described. Were we fed? Yes, a peanut butter and jelly sandwich. Were we in a home? Yes, we were sheltered. The point is that when these things happen, as I described with my stepfather, to a child, it impacts the long-term years that follow for how they see themselves.

When my mother acted the way she did, by putting us to bed early with a PB&J while frying a meal for her boyfriend, to a child, we took these acts personally.

Children always take these kinds of experiences personally and my older brother and I felt as if these bad things are happening to us, it must be because we are bad children. This is the fracturing of oneself I mentioned earlier. It creates a lifelong sense of shame. Not just in my experiences, but in a majority of those who have similar experiences when they are children.

It is important that I point out that I do not blame either my stepfather or my mother because they were simply acting out their own traumas. They were acting on the wounds that were passed down to them from their parents. In a way, we are all victims of people who were once themselves victims.

Blaming a parent has no ground when the person who suffers realizes that trauma is passed down from families for generations. As the British psychiatry John Bowlby said, "Recognition of this quickly dispels any disposition to see the parents as villain."

This is what happens in most households with these kinds of issues, as they get continuously passed on from parent to child and so forth, continuing to cycle down on an ongoing basis for multiple generations. We will always pass onto our children what we ourselves have not resolved.

Later, I found out that my stepfather was never told who his real father was and there was a tremendous amount of pain and agony he was in, particularly in the way he was raised and brought up. It's no wonder he acted like he did, as he had his own deep unresolved wounds.

Eventually that day would come when I would live with my grandparents, the mother of my mom, and learn through the process of living my teenage years with them, some of the traits and attributes of how my mom developed into who she was. It was all passed down traumas, generationally from one member of the family to the next.

Perhaps this is something familiar to you as you read this and if it is, and you are ready to break that cycle, this book will give you the tools for doing so in practical, effective, and understandable ways.

This is one of those things that escapes most of us, and we tend to not even think back to these years and as we become adults. We assume that," Well, I don't remember all that much of my childhood (especially 0-3) so, it's not that big a deal." But these years form the template or measuring device of how we view everything in regard to the rest of our life.

By the time a child turns 7 years old, they have already learned half of everything they will know the rest of their life. A brief reviewing of these two paragraphs summarized from *Pediatrics*, a journal of the American Academy of Pediatrics, from Harvard University's Center on the Developing Child, solidifies this understanding:

The architecture of the brain is constructed through an ongoing process that begins before birth, continues into adulthood, and establishes either a sturdy or a fragile foundation for all health, learning and behavior that follow.

The interaction of genes and experiences literally shapes the circuitry of the developing brain and is critically influenced by the mutual responsiveness of the adult-child relationships, particularly in early childhood years.

In my case, having a stepfather behaving violently towards us, physically beating us, constantly drinking alcohol, fighting with my mom, on top of having a mother who was emotionally unavailable is what formed the lens of how I viewed myself, how I viewed life, other people and where my place was in the world.

It was no wonder there were so many troubles I had early in life and felt the need to escape my pain through addictions. It is the earliest years of our life that form the lens of how we self-reflect on ourselves for the decades that follow.

I didn't know it at the time, but this was all happening for a reason. My childhood was preparing me for what would later become my passion and profession: resolving and reversing the impact of childhood trauma.

Now we can begin to see how the human mind matures and develops because when we are incarnated at conception in this world, for all practical purposes, we are naive, and we have no perceptions on anything that is relative of man.

Then with each moment that passes by environmental information interacts with our developing heart, brain, our nervous system and our five senses and this data begins to accumulate and organize into groups on what they have in common. This begins to form bits and pieces of perceptions on every topic, subject concept and idea received by the mind and organizes it into our lens of what becomes our reality. Later, we will go it depth on this.

We will cover the mind model soon but for now understand that your conscious mind, or the part you are aware of, differentiates situations *by time sequence.*

When you think of certain circumstances or past events you can remember the beginning of it, the middle, and the end of it. That is a feat of the conscious mind.

The more powerful subconscious mind differentiates things, not by time, but *by what they have in common.* These perceptions of similarity begin to, as more and more are accumulated, get grouped together and fall into place one at a time similar to the pieces of a jigsaw puzzle eventually building up a complete "picture" of what life is for us.

This complete jigsaw puzzle now is held in the subconscious mind, protected by a powerful barrier and will be manifested with ruthless efficiency.

It is at this moment which we learned that we are truly products of our earliest environmental conditions. All these earliest experiences which build up this jigsaw puzzle are also the most significant and influential ones of our entire adult life.

For example, my stepfather called me a fool so frequently growing up, that it's no surprise that as an adult, I always felt rather incompetent about things.

As soon as I reached the ability to pedal a bike, I attempted to spend as much time as I could far away from that house. Covering as much ground as possible, I peddled all the way across town to be around friends or be outside, exploring in nature.

Many hours were spent silently wishing for any kind of change or shift to prevent me from ever going back to that house, and when you make a request like that, you never know how the answer may come or what forces you are interacting with.

That answer did come in a very sobering and merciless way. At the age of 10, my mom had a very serious car accident. It was one of such magnitude that perhaps 1 out of 10,000 people could have survived it. Although she did survive, the rest of our lives would be forever changed, something that I had yearned for.

Additionally, she was from that point on, no longer to take care of us.

When this day of change came, I was in school having fun with friends and basking in enjoyment of being away from home and suddenly my (previous) stepfather and older brother came in to get me from school.

I had no idea what to think, as I sat in the back seat of the car in silence wondering why he was there and why he was taking me away from my classroom escape. After some silence, he said "Your mom has been in a car accident." I immediately felt sad, as any child would in this circumstance and began to cry, as I knew the situation was serious.

When we arrived at the hospital in Wagoner, Oklahoma that morning, it hit me like a cylinder block of just how serious she was when she was laying there on ventilator and swollen beyond any recognition. She was in no shape for such inadequate hospital in a small town, so she was immediately transported to Tulsa hospital.

Due to the circumstances that my older brother and I were now in, our grandparents who lived in Wichita, Kansas, came to get us. Following this, the first year after her car accident, my older brother moved in with with my grandparents, and I moved in with my aunt and uncle in Conway Springs, Ks.

My aunt and Uncle were also severe alcoholics but were not physically abusive. They had no experience with children and the transition was very awkward and I found myself spending hours alone in my room with little to no interaction with them.

They had their own routine and I found myself tagging along with them as they spent every weekend in a local bar called Bert's Place.

By the time I was 11, every single weekend was spent going Bert's Place playing pool with a guy named Earnie in a bar filled with cigarette smoke, alcoholic adults and intoxicated men who would occasionally break out with some violent episode of fighting right before my eyes.

Not even a teenager yet, I was the youngest one in this place and since my aunt knew the owners, they did their best to make me feel welcome in their own way.

As you can imagine, all these sudden changes took their toll on me and my schoolwork suffered tremendously as I was uncooperative, causing a lot of trouble, showing having very concerning behaviors in the eyes of both my peers and authority figures. All of this resulted in me being sent to a variety of counselors and even being held back and repeating the 5th grade all over again.

There were all kinds of counseling, testing and brain scans done on me over and over to see if I had any kind of mental illness or diagnostically significant brain disorders with all the conclusions finding nothing out of the ordinary.

In reality, what was occurring was the strengthening and reinforcing of an initiating event from early childhood and everything that had occurred in my earlier years. As a result, I felt more and more like a reject.

This continued for the next year before I moved in with my grandparents and my older brother. This was a relief in some sense because my grandparents didn't do any drugs or drink alcohol and lived in a nice neighborhood, something that was a new experience for me. At first, it seemed more peaceful, and they seemed to be a little nicer on the surface than the previous experiences I had known.

I found myself immediately having old patterns emerging and I felt rejected when I started going to school. My entire body was always buzzing with high level of anxiety, constantly on alert and being nervous with no end.

My cousin, who I had gotten along with when we knew each other as children, completely turned against me. Since I was now living with my grandmother, and attending the same school as her in Goddard, Kansas, she had completely changed in the way she treated me, as though I was a total outsider.

I can even recall hearing about her telling friends just how messed up I was, about the broken home that I came from and everything else. As you can imagine, this just proliferated the rejection I already felt, and on top of this, my cousin's older brother did the same thing to my older brother.

It is important to point out that this illustrates when you have an identity, or a self-image, that reflects the ways you feel about yourself, the internal beliefs that are established growing up will automatically set the tone for how other people are going to treat you, and how the environmental factors are going to reflect on you and how the universe itself will respond to you. This book will show with you compelling science of how this works and from this, give you the power to create changes in your life.

I was walking around with chaos inside of me, it proliferated into discomfort, feeling somehow, abnormal, unworthy, and deficient. As a result, I would only see, hear, feel, and experience circumstances that matched my internal feelings.

Feelings of strongly disliking school began to develop and the relief that I felt living with my grandparents was short lived, that is until the point where I experienced smoking marijuana the first time. It seemed to instantly relieve me of what had seemed a pain that never ceased.

It is at this moment where we should point out that virtually all addictions, from marijuana and alcohol, to being a workaholic, gambling, drugs, and other types of behaviors are all attempts to escape momentarily.

Keith Richards, the famous band member of Rolling Stones who had his own addictions with heroin who once said, "All the contortions we put ourselves through just not to be ourself for a few hours, "shows us that addictions are about escaping who we are and what we feel even if it's momentarily and has a great cost associated with it. I found that smoking marijuana was such a wonderful escape that I went to great lengths to find ways of getting it.

In fact, I would steal things on a regular basis from whoever I could including classmates, family members and from my grandparents. Stealing itself soon developed into an addiction and I found myself doing it on a regular basis because of the adrenaline and surge of stress hormones that recreated the feelings it gave me.

The *jolt of surging stress hormones during the act stealing was something I had grown up my entire life feeling.*

It was my "familiar" and my nervous systems operating baseline.

Just like the addict relapses, I found myself doing it more and more just to have those old familiar feelings, without any conscious awareness of why I was doing it and disregarding the consequences.

As wrong as it was and although I knew better, the feelings it gave my body were such powerful drivers that there was little to no resistance. *We will always seek out what is familiar,* as to our nervous system, familiar is interpreted as "safe", even if the behavior is completely harmful, wrong on all accounts and perhaps even dangerous.

I began stealing from wallets, purses, shopping malls, random cars parked along the road and throughout my grandparents' garage. Any items of value in the garage that I could find, I would take to pawn off.

This of course was all an attempt to feel the surge of adrenaline as well as to use the money to purchase marijuana.

I had no idea that *it was all a cycle to reproduce to feelings that felt similar to what I had felt during my entire childhood.*

The crowd of people I began to associate with were like me, with similar past traumas, who elicited similar behaviors, habits, and the same kind of destructive characteristics.

They even had the same deep-down attributes of feeling rejected by their peers. It was as if somehow, on a deep level, we matched. This pattern of being part of the wrong crowd and stealing, which continued to escalate to the severity of eventually where we would break into cars, and even houses looking for something to steal, made me feel like I belonged.

Very quickly, this haphazard behavior became a way of life from me during my high school years. Yes, that was me.

Imagine for a moment, the hypothetical example of a family. This includes a father, a mother and a teenager just walking along, enjoying a nice day at the park and they come upon another teenager to which the father stops for a moment and looks down at his teenage child and says to him or her, "Do not ever hang around that person. Understand?" That person of concern *was me* in those years and rightly so. Looking back, it was almost as if that was another life lived by a completely different person in a different realm. It was the time in my life where I was a lost soul.

The point is that I changed. It is more than possible to change if the person does what I did: make the decision to change.

I will share what that decision meant later in this chapter. However, it got worse before it got better.

It is said that for many of us to wake up, we need a wakeup call and mine simply hadn't arrived quite yet. This destructive cycle would continue all the way through the years of high school and past my graduation.

Honestly, I don't even know how I graduated with such poor work and low grades, yet it had to occur strictly based on an attendance and not academia. I graduated high school with a D average, but I still graduated.

Once I graduated, my grandparents helped get me an established apartment in west Wichita and soon I moved out and had my own place. As you can imagine, the cycle of destruction and drug addiction only proliferated.

It wasn't long before I found myself seeking out heavier drugs including methamphetamines along with the marijuana and alcohol. The pain which I had unconsciously carried for quite some time now was quite unbearable and it got to a point where I finally hit rock bottom.

I had been arrested a few times by this point and even spent a few days in jail. I knew deep down that this was truly only the beginning of things to come.

Then something inside of me snapped. I felt a growth of intuition deep down that was hungry for a change, a positive change. That growth became noticeably more obvious, although it wasn't in my head—it was from somewhere lower and deeper. It started to silently whisper to me that I was meant for something else and that this was not the path that I was supposed to go on. It told me I just needed to get away from this.

So, right then I decided that I was going to join the military, because it seemed like the only option, I could do to escape this pattern of self-destruct.

By this time, this ongoing cycle was so ingrained almost with the certainty of the sun rising and setting, every evening my acquaintances came over to my apartment, as I was the only one amongst them that had an apartment (all from my grandparents paying for it) so they chose to come hang out with me and indulge in drug use and video games for hours on end.

Listening to this new urge, I made the decision that I was going to do something drastic and escape this place, escape these drugs, escape these people, and escape everything I've ever known, which was only pain.

I made the decision to join the Marines because I knew it was the only way I could pull myself out of this deep, dark, and suffocating mess. I knew I did not have the internal strength, will power or the level of mental fortitude required to change from this pattern I was living.

In making this decision to join the Marines and make something better out of myself, I shifted everything within me and changed my identity.

It was here where I realized that one decision is all it takes to make a transition so vast that in a very short period, life will would never be the same. This was the first time I had done anything like this, with such a burning desire, to become a Marine, get myself into shape and learn about leadership that no matter what... I was going to do it.

Shortly after, I joined the Marine Corps and put 100% focus and effort into it. When you make a change like that and put all focus and dedication into something, it has a way of giving you a reflection of whatever you put into it.

Many times, when people go into the military, and they come back a better, more secure, and confident person, it's simply because they put something into it. They wanted something out of it, worked for it and they got it back. But this doesn't include the larger percentage of people who do not change and perhaps even get worse in the military.

In order for a person to have a remarkable and permeant change, the change has to be from inside, which is the labor of why I wrote this book.

For example, when I first arrived in my duty station, within the first week, I smelled the once familiar scent of marijuana being smoked somewhere close by. Right then and there I could have sought out the source and participated in it, because it was taking place right there in the barracks where I was stationed. But the identity I had transitioned into, wanted nothing to do with this, so I had no problem ignoring the scent and just moving on as if I never smelled it.

When I joined the Marines and was stationed in my unit, I began to take everything about it serious, starting with my health and physical status.

I worked out on my own time, studied nutrition, and became very fit, and eventually joined an elite group of Marines. I had several successful deployments to some of the most hostile places in the world and I achieved several high awards.

After my years of service, I knew it was time for me to leave the Marines. I was drawn to go back to my hometown, yet I was a completely different person then the one who had left.

I felt more focused, and my confidence was higher than it had ever been, although the internal chaos that I had always known, and the deep pain was still very present.

My nervous system responded like a light switch; one minute I was calm and relaxed and the next minute my heart was racing, and my palms were drenched in sweat. It would be easy to assume that these types of symptoms were common in combat veterans from battlefield experiences, but that is not accurate.

In both my own experience and in every patient, I've ever worked with who has experienced combat, it was *not* the military experiences that caused their symptoms of PTSD.

It was already present from my early childhood experiences although there were situations and events in the Marine Corps that proliferated the already present internal psychological wounds. It was simply a relive of an already present trauma.

My hometown of Wichita was really the only place that I felt that I belonged at this point, so I went back to the place I grew up, and before long, began to seek out environmental conditions that would give me the same kind of feelings that I had carried most of my life, including in the Marine Corps.

Although I never partook in any drugs during my service time, I found myself beginning to smoke marijuana again on a regular basis and found it was very calming to my nervous system and it seemed to help me sleep better. Other than this, being an illegal substance, I also never again had any urge to do anything against the law again either. I had been influenced by good leaders in my military career that I was focused on doing things that were much more honorable than my past endeavors.

However, my internal operating system had remained unchanged. It was so high strung, hypervigilant, and excessively revved up, that my nervous system was on constant setting of GO! GO! GO! I found it was very difficult to relax, a common sign of past trauma, unconscious turmoil and distress.

Seeking out high stress type of work, it wasn't long before I was working as an Emergency Room Technician (EMT) in the emergency room of hospitals as well as in the back from ambulances, going to horrific scenes and high tense situations. Again, in an attempt to reproduce those chaotic feelings that I had known my whole life without any knowing or awareness of it.

That's what we all tend to do. We will unconsciously seek out things that reproduce feelings that match what we felt as children and I had internal chaos, so I was naturally drawn towards it. I was around chaos as a kid so as an adult, I would seek it out, first as a combat veteran then later as an EMT responding to emergency conditions and unconsciously attempting to recreate the deepest down feelings I was already harboring.

Whatever happened to us first in our life including time in the womb and the first few years afterwards becomes the standard to what every experience after that is measured by.

For my nervous system to seek out and be in these conditions made me feel "normal" while attempting to relax or just sit quietly was something so foreign to my body, that it was not sustainable for me.

Clinically speaking, I have found this to be accurate in the case in my patients as well. For example, I had a female police officer seek me out for "job related PTSD." However, when we began our approach to healing her trauma and regressed her to the cause of her symptoms, we found it was from experiences of violence with a drunken volatile father during her earliest childhood years.

In fact, her life as a police officer, having worked in violent settings and environments involving domestic violence where all attempts to seek out a way to be around what was "normal" to her, without any conscious awareness of this taking place.

This eventually begins to catch up, just as a vehicle you drive on the highway would be if you set the cruise control on 7500 RPM for a long road trip across several states.

This high setting on neurological baseline and the constant bombardment of my nervous system with continuous surges of stress hormones began to take a toll on me and my health.

My anxiety was becoming more and more tense, and it caused my face to always be flush. I could tell my PTSD symptoms began to develop much worse and more intense as I was easily triggered by seemingly smaller things.

In the later chapters of this book, I will explain in detail of what causes this and how to effectively correct it.

Although I was a personal trainer as well as an EMT, having a "healthy lifestyle" eating nutritious foods, avoiding alcohol, and routinely working out while being in good physical shape—my mind was a total train wreck.

I felt tense throughout the day, no matter my efforts as I attempted to put my thoughts at ease with meditation or breathing techniques, they were very short lived. I avoided any and all drugs but found myself having to smoke marijuana at night to calm myself enough to fall sleep, something not uncommon in people who have symptoms of PTSD.

One day while working out at the gym I ran into an old friend who was a now very successful chiropractor. After some discussion, he invited me to his office where he told me a little bit about chiropractic and his profession.

He had wanted some of my advice on fitness, so I began personally training him. One day after meeting with him, I had another epiphany. It was similar to the little hunch, or growth that was in my gut and began to get my attention just like it did when I was supposed to leave the destructive life behind and become a Marine.

Receiving some encouragement from him, I decided right then that I was going to be a chiropractor, no matter what. Doing a little research on what chiropractic was, and how it specialized on placing emphasis on the body's own healing ability, as a personal trainer this resonated deeply with me. I felt that this journey of becoming a chiropractor, would offer more answers for me on how to heal my internal wounds than anything else that was available in the healing art professions.

At this time, I was married with my first wife and when I told her I was going be a chiropractor, she was kind of excited and was very skeptical because of the amount of schooling it takes. As you may have guessed from my background, I was not your typical "doctor material", if you know what I mean. Not many doctors have a background colored with trauma, criminal activities, and hard drug usage.

But it didn't really matter at this point. I had my mind made up and that's all it really takes. When you want something and you decide that you are going to do it, the universe has a remarkable way of stepping aside and assisting you on your path.

I decided to be a chiropractor, and that little whisper I had heard before began to tell me I was meant to do something else and something bigger than I had ever imagined. That little whim inside of me was reassuring me that I was going to find a way to help myself resolve this deep constant internal pain that I have carried my entire life.

CHAPTER 2

Proper Hydration

"Water links us to our neighbor in a way more profound and complex than any other." — John Thorson

"Thousands have lived without love, not one without water." — W. H. Aude

When it comes to anxiety and ways to effectively resolve it, we should start with the very basics before we head into the Godzilla sized problems. First and foremost, ensure you are properly hydrated with an adequate number of electrolytes as a first approach.

As simple as this may sound, I have witnessed this approach help many people who felt anxious, constant nervousness and/or relentless tension.

Ensuring there are adequate levels of electrolytes in your system is the first recommendation. I recommend a good source of spring water over municipal tap water and using a high-quality salt with it. To properly allow water to enter our cells, the body needs a salt or a sugar to activate the mechanisms for proper absorption.

Redmond's Real salt is a great choice, and it can be picked up in most grocery stores. I recommend starting with a small teaspoon sized amount with 16 ounces of water and just monitor how you feel.

People who sweat constantly, are generally fatigued and are always thirsty, no matter how much water they drank, are usually dehydrated.

It has less to do with how much water you drink and more about how much water you are able to absorb. So, start with this to ensure you've covered the basics of having adequate hydration and electrolytes. Your brain and nervous system both require water and electrolytes so ensuring that proper electrical conditions can occur within your neural pathways is the first and basic step we must cover before moving on.

CHAPTER 3

Starting with the Smaller of the Pressing Issues First.

"The reason man may become the master of his own destiny is because he has the power to influence his own subconscious mind."

Napoleon Hill

There is a topic we need to discuss to ensure your success with this book and the application to using the techniques you will learn.

This step to achieving success when trying something new is absolute key. It also eludes many people and ultimately leads to them being frustrated, unsuccessful and in the end, confused with the mindset of "it didn't work."

That topic is something we'll refer to as *bucket listing* and it is very important to start here if you are going to have success with these techniques and principles that you will learn later in the book.

Bucket listing, although time consuming, must be taken seriously for you to achieve success. You must start with smaller issues first that you want to clear before you begin to throw more heavy, pressing and nasty issues at the techniques you will be introduced to in later chapters.

Many people carry tremendous emotional problems that they aren't quite sure how to resolve and often, they can be confused at where to even start.

Perhaps, they start with approaches like acupuncture, energy work, maybe changing their diet, eating cleaner foods, and supplementing adaptogens and various herbs.

Many begin to incorporate meditation, or they begin a variety of breathing techniques and like many people they find this ultimately provides only short-term relief. (as in my case) Or it does not dissolve the underlying issue that they are seeking to resolve.

Why do these only provide short-term relief? Chances are there are a few reasons that were overlooked. This will all make sense when we cover the trauma mechanism in later chapters of this book.

What most people do when they begin to seek out various techniques to help them resolve their emotional baggage, whether they purchase a course or buy a book all with the hope of learning something that they will use to resolve their problems, unfortunately doesn't resolve them because they throw their *Godzilla size problems at it first.*

They read it on the print or watch it on a screen and they immediately throw their biggest, nastiest and most pressing issues at it and wonder why they have very limited-- if any success at all--in resolving their super-sized challenges.

The reason for the failure is because they are taking something they have absolutely no practice with, confidence, experience, or history of generating any success with and simultaneously fighting the thing *that they have the most practice doing.*

You see, your biggest problems are the ones your mind has had the most practice replaying over and over, so it is very familiar with the problem.

If you want to work on yourself and have success in slaying those beasts that reside as emotional turmoil's you've carried for many years, you must train differently. You must go at it with a different approach then the majority do.

This brings us to the process of forming a **bucket list**.

For this to happen, we should compare this scenario to a video game.

Imagine that the technique you just learned about is the equivalent to a level 1 character. This character is completely inexperienced, has no idea what lies ahead, yet is all enthusiastic with their brand-new entry level sword or a little magic wand.

Now this character is completely prepared and adequate for taking any monsters or bad guys they may encounter *as long as they stay in the level one zone.*

Now, imagine what would happen if you, as a level one character, wander into a level ten or twenty killing zone area. What happens next? As you can imagine it doesn't end very good for the level one character. Why?

Simply because the monsters on the more advanced level are much too big, powerful, and more experienced for the level one character to match.

The fresh, new character is too weak without adequate experience points to take on the larger sized and much tougher monsters that are on higher levels.

This scenario is exactly why people have no success when they first learn a new technique and they throw their biggest, heaviest, and most challenging emotional problem at it as soon as they learn it.

So, to solve this problem, let's go back to the video game metaphor. If the level one-character stays in the level one area long enough, they begin to gain valuable experience points every time they slay a monster or a bad guy on their appropriate level.

As this occurs over and over, they soon begin to level up. Before long, that level 1 character becomes a level 2 character. Soon, after the process is repeated enough times, they become a level 3 character. Next, after more experience, they become a Level 4 and so on.

Following this approach, it won't be long before that character can wander into a level 5 zone and have success with disposing of level 5 monsters.

You see? It is simply because the character is within an appropriate range for taking on the monsters in the game.

This is the exact approach you need to take when you begin this journey on attempting to reverse your PTSD, anxiety and/or emotional challenges.

If you are seeking to achieve long term success, you must begin to slay the simple and more minor issues first which is where bucket listing comes in.

To properly bucket list is equivalent to building your character up so you can slay the bigger and larger scale monsters later.

The first thing you do is a mind dump. This means that you carefully and methodically take everything that bothers you, no matter what it is, and write it down on a piece of paper as soon as you can think of it. Anything that you want to change, for any reason no matter how large or small it is, just write it all down.

Write everything down you want to change and the more you list, the better. Everything from a phobia to spiders, a past troubled divorce, your demanding boss, the annoying neighbor, or your mother in-law that always seems to push your buttons in just the way that triggers you. It doesn't matter whatever it is. Write it all down.

When you have a decent sized list of things, from 5 to 25 or more, the next step is to assign a number value next to each one of the listed problems.

The number ranking is meant to scale each one from a 1 (least intense) to a 10 (the most intense) on how intense your emotional charge or fear is in relation to the situation you wrote.

So, let's say you have known someone who just gets your blood boiling, sort of speak. Write their name down and ask yourself, "Where do I rank them on a scale of 0 to 10?" and place that number next to their name.

Look at other events and circumstances in your life and repeat the entire process. It could have been a divorce, loss of a business or an angry power tripped boss at work. Whatever it is, write it down and rank it on the scale.

The next step is to rearrange the list. Placing them in order from the least intensive (similar to the level one character in the video game) level ones and twos and increase from there to the more intensive ones.

Remember this is of vital importance because when you start working with the techniques I outline in this book, beginning with all your level one issues first and then level two challenges and clear them out using the techniques. Then the level threes and fours and so forth.

By the time you hit fives and sixes you're going to build up such an intense history of success with that technique your neurology is going to say, "Oh I can do that! I can do that!" You just keep going up the scale until you're doing the eights, nines and tens. Your nervous system and subconscious mind work off repetition, just like learning to tie a show or ride a bicycle. This is no different.

Simply doing two or three is not going to give you the history, so take your time and do the smaller levels first.

Eventually, you will find the process will start to automate and through the entire training sequence the perceived level of difficulty will not even be obvious. As you begin to take on and successfully clear the deeper rooted and heavier levels of emotional wounds, your trust and confidence grows.

The intensity between the ones and twos will be of no more significance than the eights, nines and tens on your scale of intensity.

This is exactly how it works!

The key to having success with these very powerful techniques you'll learn in this book, is to bucket list your challenges.

Here's another bonus: just the very act of creating the list and ranking them by their intensity will cause you to process this experience differently.

Doing this action takes you out of the experience and begins the process of giving you control over it. **You don't have to know all of the past experiences or sources to your anxiety for this to work** but know that listing them out and ranking them takes you from associated to dissociated state and now equips you with the power to start processing it right away.

Although some proponents of trauma work do dissociative work, it is not the long-term answer. *Disassociating from an issue is not the same as fully resolving the issue* so keep that in mind.

CHAPTER 4

The Mechanism of Trauma

"In order to change, people need to become aware of their sensations and the way that their bodies interact with the world around them. Physical self-awareness is the first step in releasing the tyranny of the past." – Bessel van der Kolk

Now that I've shared a brief history of my own childhood experiences let's examine the underlying mechanism of what some highly respected experts say is responsible for at least 8 out of 10 doctor visits in our society; the mechanism of childhood trauma.

Dr Gabor Mate explained during a lecture he gave; he asked the audience members to participate in showing how relevant this link was.

He asked them to raise their hands if within the previous five years they had visited a "neurologists, cardiologist, respirologist, rheumatologist, gastroenterologist, dermatologist, immunologist or any other kind of medical-ologist" (quotes are his words).

Then he observed many hands going up. He continued by inquiring further for them to keep their hands up if these specialists asked them about childhood stressors, childhood trauma, the relationship with their parents, expressions or experiences of joy and anger, how they feel about life itself and how they feel about themself. He noted that in a room packed with hundreds of people, the number of elevated hands remaining could be counted on the fingers of one hand. It is these unasked questions, the good doctor pointed out, that have everything to do with why most of the audience sought out the medical help in the first place.

Let us take a moment to examine and define the word trauma a little more specifically.

In this book, we will define **trauma** *as an unhealed psychological wound that is lodged in the mind and body and persists over great time and when touched, gets retriggered or activated as if it is occurring in the present moment.*

Trauma is much more common than most people recognize, and it has become something of a catchword, thrown around loosely and repeated so often that the recognition of it escapes the radar of most health care professionals and virtually all other domains in society.

The marks of trauma are so commonly ingrained into our society and culture that it is displayed in some of the most popular TV shows and completely missed by a majority of people watching them. It is so ordinary in our culture that to find someone without having been impacted by trauma would be a very rare anomaly!

The Greek definition of trauma is for a *wounding*. A psychological trauma is a wound that is sustained after the initial event and it continues to behave like a wound long after its initial encoding, or the moment of overwhelm a has occurred.

It can easily persist for a lifetime. It constricts the person's psyche, demising their view of life, of themself, inhibiting their ability to perceive beauty, wonder and gratitude (2).

Trauma restricts us from fully expressing ourselves to the highest degree. It does this by giving us an altered, distorted, cracked lens from which we view the world.

This distorted view colors and skews our perceptual interaction with the world to almost always expect the worst-case scenario. It draws our mind to have an affinity to seeing the worst interpretation of even the most anodyne circumstances. Since you are a powerful non-physical being composed of quantum particles who creates you own reality, (More on this later) healing your wounds of trauma are imperative if you are going to change your life. To transform yourself means learning to train and condition your mind to look for the positive of even some of the worst-case scenarios. To accomplish this, we must release the past, heal the wounds, the anxiety and reoccurring symptoms of Post-Traumatic Stress Disorder.

Metaphorically, like any injury, it is raw, swollen, displays heat and redness and if touched, it causes pain.

Decades later if anything comes into our life which reminds us of this, it hurts just as much as it did when we originally incurred the wound.

This chapter will detail the theories of this precise mechanism and later in the book, you will learn practical step by step processes for easily and permanently eliminating these unhealed wounds.

Another thing that could happen to these psychological wounds is that over time they begin to scar over, especially with repeated, severe traumas and scar tissue has distinct characteristics.

It is thicker than normal tissue, hence the term, "He has thick skin" when describing someone who has endured many tough emotional circumstances.

Scar tissue has no nerve endings so there's little to no feeling in people who have been traumatized as they are disconnected from their feelings. Scar tissue is rigid and lacks any flexibility, so traumatized individuals lose the kind of emotional *response flexibility* that happens when a stressful situation later arises in life.

When a stressful situation happens, traumatized people tend to react in dysfunctional or exaggerated ways.

Scar tissue also no longer grows as healthy tissue does. People who are traumatized during their childhood years tend to be stuck in specific emotional states that share very similar characteristics of their developmental process of when they were being traumatized.

Peter Levine refers to this occurrence as the *Tyranny of the Past*. It is when a stressful event happens in the present moment, and we instantly react as if we're back there in the past when this initial event first happened.

Suddenly we are no longer in the present moment at all. It happens more often than we may realize and impacts everything in our daily lives without us knowing it. From constant arguments in relationships, the sabotaging of dreams and goals, chronic illness, or even in a fit of road rage. What would cause this reoccurring phenomenon?

The problem is *it's not the past wound that's haunting us. It is how the mind and body stored the experience.* That's the real issue.

Dr Gabor Mate describes it best when he says that trauma is not what happened to you, but it is what happens inside of you as a result of the trauma. The wound that trauma causes is a process of freezing consciousness when we are overwhelmed with an emotional experience that we are unable to cope with or mentally handle.

Knowing this, lets expand on the word trauma and add more to the term: a self-hypnotic state, or a psycho-neurophysiological disassociation that, just like we mentioned before, acts and behaves like a persistent wound.

People are quite remarkable at this feat in times of great physical distress or extremely emotionally overwhelming moments and can survive those experiences because of the ability to pause the flow of consciousness and store it as a trance state.

For example, a child watching their mother and father fight can be a frightening experience. They feel overwhelmed, petrified and momentarily, freeze the millisecond when they are at the peak of neurological arousal, and store it within or around the vicinity in their body.

These pockets of "stuck energy" become embedded within our energy field, both inside and outside our body and carry the vibrational blueprint of everything within that millisecond. They only show up an occasional flash within our mind when revived along with the associated feelings of whatever was present when it was first encoded, and they are revived throughout our life in response to any environmental incident even vaguely similar to the original imprint.

A trauma imprint, or wound as we termed it earlier, is an emotional spike in our nervous system that is captured when there's a certain level of neurological arousal and stored and can be revived at any time.

To put this into perspective, imagine a scale resembling a ruler that is marked from zero (lowest) all the way to ten which would be the highest.

Let's now say that zero represents the lowest level of neurological arousal, which would be a very relaxed, almost sleep like state. Contrast that with nine representing the maximum level of emotional arousal our nervous system can handle and ten on the scale would be beyond the capacity our nervous system can handle before death occurs.

Trauma Mechanism

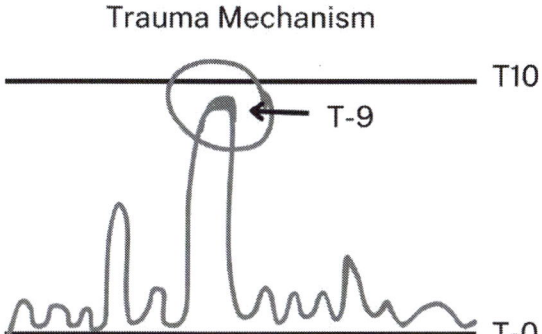

Drawing to represent Trauma mechanism

Now, think of the circuit breaker on a house during a thunderstorm. Suddenly lightning strikes the transformer on the telephone pole and in an instant, the enormous level of electricity overwhelms the house's circuit board, sparks fly everywhere, and the power goes out.

How? The lightening was too excessive for the house's ability to handle that level of electricity. In the same way, an overwhelming experience can cause an excessive level of neurological stimulation in our nervous system.

So, by this regard, if we hit ten on the scale (like the example of the house losing power), we would die. Yet, the amazing thing is that we do not reach ten. Our body has an amazing built-in protective system which prevents us from dying as a result of having an overwhelming, or traumatic experience.

It is a natural coping mechanism that temporary allows one to "disconnect" from their mind and body. In my case, I could not have survived my childhood horrors by staying present in the moment-by-moment experience and fully taking in what was happening during the times of being physically beat with a belt or a wooden paddle. The same mechanism takes place when a young child has their boundary violated by being sexually abused, or if they are witnessing something that their young immature nervous system simply cannot handle at that moment.

Now, let's shift our attention back to the zero to ten scale. Throughout our lives, we experience different levels of neurological arousal. Think of a tracking system on this scale constantly monitoring the progressive activity as it goes up and down, but it stays within normal range of what our nervous system can handle.

This up and down tracking represents our emotional highs and lows throughout our day-to-day experiences. Waking up in the morning, getting ready for the day, driving in heavy traffic on the way to work, interacting with people, having the occasional flat tire, stewing from an argument with a family member, meeting deadlines on our work assignments, our boss breathing down the back of our neck or our children yelling at each other over whose turn it is to play the video game or who was in the bathroom the longest are just examples of these highs and lows we inevitably face with ordinary routine life.

As you can imagine, these produce varying levels of neurological arousal, and this is equivalent to the tracking system increasing and decreasing on that zero to ten scale. As long as the range of the tracking system stays within the" normal" operating range, let's say between 1 and 3, 4 or 5, everything functions smoothly.

Everyone has their own levels of sensitivity and unique perception therefore this scale and the stimuli that causes levels of arousal and ultimately what we will call trauma is relative to the individual. An event that traumatizes one person may not traumatize another who witnesses the same event.

However, one concept is incredibly consistent: the younger and less secure the individual is, the more susceptible and vulnerable they are to being traumatized.

When an incident occurs that breaks the normal operating range of neurological functioning, it creates a sudden spike in the intensity and is enough to break the threshold, thus creating a millisecond escalation of shock near the top of the scale.

As this occurs, just before the moment the increasing spike of arousal reaches 9 on the scale, the moment before the critical maximum level of 10, something remarkable happens within our nervous system. (Remember if we hit 10, we die. Think back to the house losing power when lightning struck)

A trauma protective mechanism immediately activates and for a fraction of a second, everything goes offline.

Ever had a moment of slow motion during a very overwhelming experience? A near fatal mistake driving a car, witnessing a horrific accident, or receiving a very disturbing phone call?

That slow motion moment is your nervous system momentarily *freezing* the flow of consciousness. Everything within that moment of consciousness is shut off and the nervous system zips that precise millisecond, including all the feelings, the overwhelm, the pain, the environmental context--sight, sounds, smells, tastes, etc. — all of the trauma and seals it into a holographic container which can be stored somewhere inside, outside or throughout our body.

Our body is capable of doing this feat, as in a way of saying, "Well, since you do not have the emotional capacity, or capability to handle this moment, (such as a young child fighting back or running from someone violating their boundaries), I will store this for you so you can go back later and process this to its full completion."

In the example of the child mentioned above, the best-case scenario for this child would be to escape or fight back against the misuse of their body. I call it the best-case scenario because had the child been able to utilize anger to prevent the violation of their boundaries, the trauma may have been prevented.

Although the emotional arousal from such a conflict would have certainly elevated, the highest peak moment is when a sense of *powerlessness*, whereabouts, even the best utilization of actions or resources cannot seem to prevent what is about to occur to us.

To a small child, these options of fighting or running away are not easily available as either one could further place them in danger. Therefore, this built-in protective mechanism defaults to its only option: *storing and suppressing* this very moment by tuning out the emotions involved and locking them into a freeze response where fight and flight are not possible (3).

When we have an experience that hurts us so badly that we need to react shut down or avoid it, our tendency is to disregard what we feel. An emotional split takes place within us that all too often evolves into a coping mechanism where we repress down the emotions surrounding what we've experienced and bury it somewhere deep inside of our body to keep it from potentially causing more pain.

The problem is that pain doesn't go away. It just resides in a place of our body where we store it.

Oftentimes when we least expect, it reemerges showing itself in an unpredictable unimaginable way, usually as a trigger which restimulated the buried pain.

Psychologist Rollo May once pointed out that humans have the ability to the pause between a stimulus from the environment and the response that we give it, to decide which way we wish to "throw our weight." This stored holographic imprint that behaves like a wound and its capacity to be triggered *removes that capability of pausing.*

This capability of allowing us to pause before we respond is called **response flexibility**. This determines how we adjust through the ebbs and flows that life brings us. When we are traumatized that ability to pause before we respond between a stimulus and an action is stolen from us.

Improving functionality of this response flexibility, is amongst the first noticeable changes we will see in our lives when we begin to utilize the techniques that are outlined later in this book.

Overtime, without addressing these stored holographic wounds, the internalized feelings of guilt, shame, fear, anger, and resentment may result in the inability to contain the increasing experiences of similar emotional situations which eventually cause a breakdown of the person's psyche.

For example, drug addictions, alcoholism or even bouncing around from relationship to relationship, including being unfaithful to a spouse, produce more shame and guilt in the individual. This in turn amplifies the feelings that the person is trying to mask by their behaviors and/or self-medicate.

Eventually this pattern leads to hitting "rock bottom" where the marijuana, the alcohol, the drugs, and other unhealthy defenses including denial all break down. This moment is one of the main ways that our subconscious mind begins to deploy any means necessary, from a loss of a job to tumors, for the person to become consciously aware that something buried deep down needs attention.

Like a beach ball in a swimming pool, the deeper and more forceful we attempt to suppress this ball of unresolved emotion under the water the more the pressure increases forcing it to the surface.

Let's go back to the example of the house. Unlike the house, which lost power, we are capable of surviving traumatic overwhelming moments simply because we have the ability of capturing an entire traumatic event and reducing it down to a hologram like structure and storing it in any neuron within the body.

According to Karl Pribram, a neuroscientist from Stanford University, consciousness itself is holographic and fractal. All five of our senses operate this way, as do our memories of traumatic overwhelm.

The permeant memory stored in our subconscious mind retrieves meaning in our world by projecting or expanding it at various frequencies through a three-dimensional living pattern called a **hologram**.

A hologram is produced when a single coherent light such as a laser is split into two separate beams of light. One of the most famous examples of a hologram comes Artoo Detoo from the movie Star Wars.

The first beam is bounced from the object that is intended to be photographed, such as Princess Leia's character in the movie Star Wars. The second beam is aimed at a reflected surface such as a mirror and then displayed as an interference pattern on a holographic plate. The resulting display created a three-dimensional image of a woman's sculpture of light asking for Obi Wan Kenobi to help her.

World leading quantum physics expert David Bohm, a protege of Albert Einstein and the physicist from the University of London, as well as Pribram, both have independently concluded that the universe, our nervous system and our brains function as a giant, complex interconnected hologram. (4).

Additionally, Pribram points out that all our memories, including our traumatic ones, are structured similar to this holographic model which are composed of billions and billions of tiny fragments of light that make up a holographic imprint.

Understand that each individual tiny fragment of the hologram, contains the entire image, or in this case memory.

The piece, no matter how small, is equal to the whole. There is evidence put forth that everything in our world--from grains of sand to dust, feathers, planets and electrons that move the speed of light are also 3 dimensional projections produced on a level of reality far beyond our own conscious understanding.

This also means that our physical bodies are not as the "solid" flesh robotic structures that we were once conditioned to see them as being. This will make much more sense as we continue to the next chapters and even more so when we begin the process of clearing these out as described later.

In many years of doing subconscious change work on both myself and my patients, it was this concept that I did not understand, that limited my progress in most (not all) cases.

Although there would be some kind of positive shift momentarily, the previous approaches often left fragments of the holographic impression composed of the traumatic imprint behind.

Once that fragment was triggered from environmental stimuli, because it contained the entire memory, the old feelings returned once again. This means that the traumatic wound was still there and the pain, was still stored.

To better understand this structure, imagine a container full of water. Now, imagine dropping three pebbles into the water and as they collide with the surface, ripples are created on the surface. As the ripples radiate outward towards the rim of the container, imagine the surface of the water is instantly frozen. As you can image, the outward ripple pattern is preserved instantly in the sheet of frozen ice.

If we removed the frozen surface and then exposed it to a powerful coherent source of light, like one from a laser, we would create a three-dimensional representation of the position of the pebbles, the speed at which they fell, the surface structure of the three pebbles, the weight of the pebbles, the temperature, any sound they made as they hit the surface and any other details regarding the pebbles. It is all recorded in that ripple pattern frozen in ice.

This is what causes a traumatic memory to seem so real to the person who re-experiences it. Whatever sensory data was happening at the time of the overwhelm, is all still present in that pocket of consciousness.

If a veteran during his time in Iraq, for instance, was present when an IED (Improvised explosive device) exploded and within a millisecond, created tremendous force, crashing sounds, impacts from that force and a crushing pain from pieces of the Humvee exploding, everything in that instant is recorded and stored somewhere in or around his body.

If he survives, yet happens to lose a limb during the trauma, yet the memory container was stored as a hologram like structure, all it takes is the memory to go active, by getting triggered and all the pain to return—even if the physical limb is gone. This is known as phantom limb pain.

Every fraction of data picked up by that person's five senses is recorded, to the slightest minute detail—just like the ice recorded the data from pebbles.

Viewed another way, consider the story of Sue, a patient of mine who came to me for chronic headaches and PTSD. Her past was clouded from domestic violence from her former husband, who was a violent alcoholic.

For years, Sue was the target of violent fits of rage and on one particular occasion, he suddenly lashed out to hit her face. At that moment, every bit of the surrounding environmental data was instantly recorded in her energy field and subconscious mind as a holographic-like container of memory.

The background setting, the lights, the sounds and smell, including where he struck her — are all recorded and captured in a pocket of consciousness composed of billions of fragments, each one containing all the fear, the pain, the overwhelm and all other emotions that were present in that precise moment.

During this particular moment of his rage, when he had assaulted her, in the background, the television was on. At the millisecond of her nervous systems overwhelm, the television was playing a particular commercial for a certain sport drink; it was amongst that data captured in that holographic memory.

In other words, an entire traumatic event, whether it is from a veteran in Iraq, a woman who experienced a bout of domestic violence, or anything else the mind and nervous system interprets as life threatening, can be captured and stored only to be retrieved when anything resembling the original moment of encoding is encountered.

Moreover, it does not always have to be associated with violent encounters or associated with battlefields.

Sue's memory was stored in a particular area of her body without her having any awareness of it. When she contacted me, she had already left this man because of the abuse, and yet, despite being away from him for a year, she found herself suffering from flashbacks and headaches.

When I was inquiring with her about the flashbacks, she recalled a moment when she was watching television and without warning, she is suddenly in a full out panic as her nervous system was triggered. In her mind, his face flashes. The pain from his fists returns in the areas where he hit her. She is sobbing and feels in full threat mode as if her life is in danger.

When we further investigated this moment using regression work, it turned out that in the background on the television, the commercial for that same sport drink came onto the screen which triggered her panic attack.

As you can imagine, the stress that this ongoing cycle plays on our human physiology is immense.

A 2019 study conducted in Cancer Research indicated that women who have severe Post-Traumatic Stress Disorder were observed to have twice the risk of ovarian cancer as women with no history of a traumatic exposure [5].

The publication from Harvard University known as the Daily Gazette further reports, "the findings indicate that having higher levels of PTSD symptoms such as being easily startled by ordinary noises or avoiding reminders of the traumatic experience can be associated with increased risk of ovarian cancer even decades after women experience the traumatic event."

We are capable of capturing an entire traumatic experience and reducing it into a "container" stored in or around the body that may lie dormant until a stimulus triggers the holographic data. This is the fundamental principle that outlines the reoccurring theme that individuals with PTSD routinely experience.

A part of your body that becomes tense, tight, or uncomfortable on certain environmental cues gives you a glimpse of this. Ever get a vice like headache when your mother-in-law is coming over? How about nausea before giving a presentation before a crowd of people? The evidence is clear that emotional stressors are inseparable from the physical states of our bodies in both illness and in health.

Consider a patient of mine who said she had asthma. When I asked her when she notices the asthma attacks the most, she replied, "…when I drive over bridges." It is very clear that there is a memory component involved in this, but it is not uncommon.

Allergies have a tremendous mind and body interaction. For example, if a person is allergic to roses and you show them a plastic rose, they will have an allergic response (6).

If that is not already intriguing enough, James Oschman points out in his book *Energy Medicine, The Scientific Basis* that the frequencies that are emitted from a person's body during an allergic response are fully capable of triggering a spontaneous allergic reaction in another person who is already susceptible to allergies.

On a more serious note, memory-based experiences are the underlying mechanism of how PTSD impact the person who had experienced trauma, or overwhelm, and the wound from it — a holographic imprint — brings back all the hurt associated with it when it is triggered.

Post-traumatic stress disorder is a conditioned encoding a variety of symptoms including pain originating with a traumatic event in such a way that it revives a recurrence of the original symptoms. These symptoms can vary from nightmares, flashbacks, phobia type reactions, hypervigilance, hyperactive sensitivities to various sensory stimuli (smells, bright lights, etc.) tightness, tension, or discomfort in certain areas of the body and/or, high levels of irritation when some levels of the original traumatic stimuli are triggered.

In the same way, if a person has experienced PTSD symptoms from an encounter where they felt like their life was diminished or altered in some way and they go through therapy, similar to Emotional Freedom Technique (EFT), or Eye Movement Desensitization and Reprocessing (EMDR), and although there may be improvements, the person may still experience reoccurring symptoms after the therapy. The chances for reoccurring triggers of the original encoding are still present.

Why?

Because although the holographic imprint maybe getting addressed or desensitized, it is often reduced, but not completely neutralized so there are remaining fragments left behind. Once a fragment is triggered at a later time, those symptoms, such as pain or anxiety also return. Additionally, the Initial Sensitizing Event was also likely not resolved using these methods.

Note: I have training in both of these techniques, including EMDR's predecessor, Eye Movement Integration(EMI).

I am fully aware of the variety of scale that people present with under the umbrella label of PTSD. It's also worth noting that in the British Journal of Psychiatry in 2005 pointed out a remarkable finding that people undergoing certain "life events" that were assumed to be ordinary stresses and emotional hardships such as relationship challenges, family issues and problems associated work did not qualify for a formal diagnosis of PTSD.

However, these people *suffered more* PTSD like symptoms including emotional numbing, hypervigilance, and insomnia than the more obviously traumatized people who had battlefield experience or survived environmental disasters.

It is not the scope of this book to diagnose any individual who has been experiencing any above-mentioned symptoms. That must be done by a licensed professional.

It is the scope of this book for helping a person understand the mechanisms for reoccurring symptoms, panic attacks, anxiety and the nature of the holographic imprints that occur at moments of overwhelm in their life and therefore understanding how to completely neutralize those holographic imprints.

The way to completely reverse these imprints, or other undesired impacts from them, is to *completely neutralize* and *cancel all fragments of the hologram* through something known in physics as **Destructive Interference**. During the technique phases in this book, you will observe this in yourself.

Destructive interference is when the waves of certain patterns of opposite amplitude collide and result in no amplitude at that point as the two waves of opposite amplitude cancel each other out.

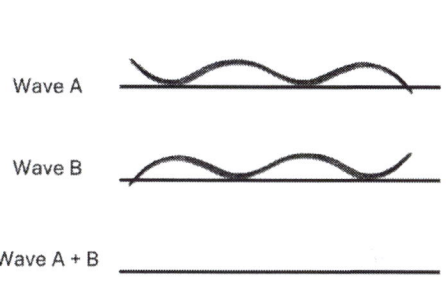

Destructive Interference

Wave A

Wave B

Wave A + B

Not only is this how noise cancelling headphones work, but it is also how we cancel out the holographic imprint from trauma that has been encoded in or around our body.
This will be explained in much more detail when we begin the techniques later chapters. They are based on the *holographic principle that nature creates tremendous change in large systems very quickly.*

To summarize, a hologram is a way of storing immense amounts of data so each individual part, is equal to the whole.

The holographic principle is what happens when you hear a song and it brings back a flash of a childhood experience, or an event such as prom. A smell of certain foods, like apple pie, may bring back a memory of your grandmother's house. Driving on a familiar road that you have not visited in years, suddenly takes you back to the moments you spent on or near that road. I think you get the idea.

This phenomenon happens because some form of stimuli (including a random thought) from the environment triggered a fragment of that hologram. It may be triggered by an outside event, or it can be triggered by an inside flashback of a past memory.

We, as humans, go in and out of memories anywhere from 15 to 50 times a minute and we do this on a regular basis. Think about how many times your mind takes a trip while you are walking down a sidewalk or driving down a long highway.

If you revisit a memory of a time when you were embarrassed, and the feelings and emotions come up, your brain wave instantly goes into the same pattern and your physiology matches exactly how it was when the incident occurred.

The memory is equivalent to a holographic complex that is sealed into a little pocket dimension and the problem is that it's now running and operating on an endless loop. It stored everything that took place up to the moment it reached level 9, before this point in time and nothing beyond it. In other words, this stored pocket dimension *does not know the event is over*.

Imagine a soldier or a Marine who is no longer in the battlefield or fire fight but is at their childhood home with friends and family around them and they are having a barbeque. There is a deeper part of that soldier who that still "thinks" that the battle is taking place, which causes him or her to be more on guard, even in a safe environment.

That means this fragment of consciousness knows everything that you knew up to level 9 and nothing beyond it. Your unconscious mind doesn't know the overwhelming experience is over!

This is the mechanism behind Post Traumatic Stress Disorder because if something in the environment retriggers a single fragment of the stored hologram, instantly, to the subconscious mind, the event is happening all over, and we are no longer in the present time.

We now understand from research using single photon emission computed tomography scanners that we go back into the initial brain wave pattern and same state of physiological distress as we did at the moment of original encoding when the trauma first occurred.

In other words, our neurology cannot tell the difference between the memory of the event, from the actual event itself, even if there's decades of time between the two.

In looking at the source of trauma, there is often a misunderstanding when we use the word trauma to describe something. To better understand this, we must be clear in our definition of trauma because when we think of trauma, we tend to think about horrible things such as car crashes, war zones and sexual molestation and all these horrid things. In some ways it is accurate to do so.

However, we also need to expand our understanding of trauma to mean anything the nervous system views as life threatening. Even if it's getting your toy taken away when you're a 2-year-old at a vital moment. Even if it's your parents yelling at each other in front of you when you are an infant.

It can even be less obvious events such as being alone in a room or in a room with people and nobody's playing with you. An infant born into a loveless marriage where the father (or mother) is having an affair even before he's born is also a traumatic event for the infant. As you will read about our non-physical nature later in upcoming chapters, it will become more obvious to understand how an infant mind can "sense" these kinds of things, such as emotional states that a person, including a nearby parent, are in.

Don't make the assumption that they are too young to be influenced by parents fighting nearby, tremendous worry about the finances, or one of the parents having an affair. These scenarios have come up numerous times with my patients' involving incidents from their infancy.

Trauma can also originate as one major event that happens, or it can be an accumulation of events, or smaller traumatic occurrences that all have a similar resonance.

British American anthropologist Ashley Francis Montagu wrote a book called *Touching the Human Significance of the Skin* that emphasizes how important touch is for the proper brain development in infants and children.

If you're not being held enough as a baby or not being touched, this is a deprivation for development. Being held close, touched, and comforted with human touch is so important for human brain development and not being held is itself a traumatic event for infants.

We are all born needing assistance, needing to be understood, to be attuned with from a parental figure, to be seen, to have our emotions received and validated. This one of the essential needs of children. Infants and young children can be traumatized *not just by terrible things* happening to them *but just by not having their needs met*. This means by not being seen, not being heard, and not being held, are also traumatizing events that are often overlooked and misunderstood.

The point is that for childhood trauma to occur, you don't necessarily need terrible things to happen to you.

This is the most difficult area for people to understand in regard to this definition. Most people, including degreed professionals, misunderstand this by assuming that for a traumatic event, you need horrific events to occur.

That is true. Horrific events can be very traumatizing to infants, toddlers, and children. However, you can wound a child just because the parents are too stressed, disengaged emotionally, and unavailable to really see the child for who they are.

Additionally, trauma to an infant or child can occur when good things, which were meant to occur never did. The most common ones I have witnessed are absences of emotional soothing, having an emotionally available parent during critical points in life or even the act of being welcomed in a parent's presence.

To the developing human nervous system, these things are just as trauma inducing as war zones and in most cases, they are the root cause for people who reach out to me.

It is important to point out that one side of this is paradoxical and perhaps even a bit unnerving or scary and the other side is amazingly liberating. That is: everybody who suffers from trauma is *not broken*. They can certainly feel that way. God knows they feel that way.

Yet, when you're manifesting symptoms from long standing repressed emotions, it is the sign of a *properly functioning nervous system*. As hard as this may be for some to believe, it is a testament of how amazing our body is at surviving the initial overwhelming event.

It's just nobody in our society, including the medical system or academia, teaches us the dynamics of the system so we do not know what to do when the system did what it was programmed to do. Nobody taught you how to go back and reprocess those events so that the trapped energy of those occurrences is decompressed correctly.

This book will guide you on practical do-it-yourself steps to locate these in your own body and mind, observe them and clear them from your nervous system which will allow those past "wounds" to heal. Even if you do not remember the source of it, this is not necessary to clear them out. If you can access one point of the holographic imprint, you can change the entire construct.

For healing to occur, _the following paragraphs are vital to understand_: After doing the **Holographic Deletion & Holographic Reframing** to yourself, which is a simple, yet powerful technique used to heal past wounds, you may notice after the session, emotions and feelings come up.

That is okay and normal! You must let them.

That's the body shedding and releasing repressed energy. The technique itself is fast, yet the processing goes on afterwards for a week or maybe more. Through the holographic principle, nature creates tremendous change very quickly.

If uncomfortable feelings come up after the session, the first thing most people tend to do is try to stuff it down, avoid it, distract themselves, deny them or mentally argue with them.

Why? It is what they've been used to doing for the past years instead of letting it come up and out. *As it comes up, it also comes out!!*

My mentor once said, "As you feel it, you reveal it. As you reveal it, you heal it." <u>That repressed energy must leave the body</u> and often times we have the same uncomfortable feelings come up (especially after we do this work) we had when the trauma occurred.

If you let it process out, it's gone! It's *when you try to stuff it down and do everything but let yourself feel it fully, that you prolong it, or you actually make it worse.*

For every unit of energy, you try to keep locked in the body, you need an equal or greater amount of energy to keep it there! If you are constantly accumulating more emotional weight, you're essentially adding more and more emotional energy to keep it there. After this cycle continues over and over, what do you think happens?

You only have a finite capacity before these repressed emotions transition into physical symptoms and eventually chronic conditions. This will all make more sense as we cover more depths into this subject.

CHAPTER 5

The Mind Model

"Trauma is a fact of life. It does not, however, have to be a life sentence. Not only can trauma be healed, but with appropriate guidance and support, it can be transformative." – Peter A. Levine

Let's begin to discuss the details in understanding the parts of the mind and the functions of each and how they work. Because all the good changes we want in our lives begins once we understand how to better understand this wonderful part of us.

The mind is not the brain simply because the *mind extends beyond the physical organ* of the brain. Think of the mind being action of the brain.

To introduce this action, consider the findings involving researchers in 2014 from the Star Lab Institute Axiom Robotics and Harvard Medical School. When they published their findings, it shocked their peers.

In their experiments they had proven that they could detect and identify exact words from the thoughts coming out of the subjects' brains. It was an amazing revelation. It opened up new possibilities of brain-to-brain communication as the researchers successfully transmitted a message from a person sitting in France to a person sitting in India, without the subjects even typing or saying a word. The foundation for how this is possible will be explained in further chapters in this book.

With an understanding of the mind model, we can look at life through this graph and see a much clearer picture of what's going on. We will start to see the specifics on what causes chronic illness in people's lives. We will also see what's discovered when a chronic pain sufferer, that one doctor has given up on, is healed through a process that properly applies the applications of this model.

If you've never heard this before, now is the time to fully grasp this statement: *The mind is the body's controlling force* and all areas.

Hippocrates himself said that the body's natural tendency is towards health. Said another way, the body will naturally continue to function in a way that self-healing, self-lubricating, and self-correcting. This statement completely makes sense and is agreed upon by most people, yet it's right here where Western medicine takes an interesting turn in its approach. While this tendency is naturally driven towards health and it's interfered with, medical approaches, including most functional medicine practitioners today, look *outward* at the physical body for the interference.

What ancient wisdom and modern day understanding of the mind tells us is that the interference *originates from the inside* not the outside. This approach is often taught in chiropractic colleges as well as the interference is spinal misalignments known as subluxations. As a chiropractor myself I have found that this approach in some ways aligns with the medical model of looking at the interference as an outside force rather than an inside force.

It's the mental body that's the causative factor on the inside force which I'm referring to.

As every wise person, great teacher and healer throughout time including Hippocrates has mentioned, that it's the inside world which influences our outside world.

In other words, it's thought that creates our destiny. If things go wrong in our life including our health, it's an act of mind that is responsible.

Let's look closer at this mind model and start to understand how the mind, body and spirit worked together to affect health. I will be using very simple illustrations to help you visualize this mind model better. Be sure to take some time to animate these graphics of your mind and how it works and review this mind model slowly and repeatedly. I have found tremendous success with my patience because of the power packed explanation for life happenings as they understand this mind model.

You may notice that as you learn the model and begin to use the techniques together it starts out quite mechanical.

As we master the mechanics, and you begin to have success with your bucket list that we discussed in the last chapter it initially becomes very tool like.

As you develop skills with the tool, you'll notice a playful friendship begins to develop. This friendship only grows into something more purposeful and powerful. As this friendship continues to grow one day, you'll notice that it's brought you closer to God than ever. That is a wonderful experience and moment for the self-healer.

From the illustration you will notice that we see the conscious mind as the top smaller circle that is located inside of the bigger circle that represents the Subconscious mind. The way this illustration represents the conscious mind shields the subconscious mind from the outside influence.

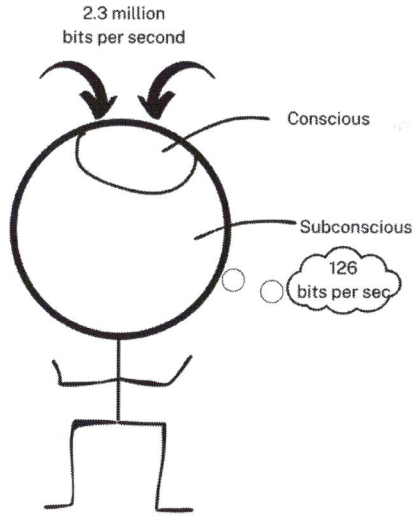

The arrows indicate sensory data as well as a vast amount of information that flows through the entire body and it's very important to realize that even though it appears from the drawing that the conscious mind receives it first, we must understand that the conscious mind *is the least informed last to know part of us.*

In other words, by the time we have a conscious thought (anything we are aware of) it has already completely passed through and been screened by all parts of the subconscious mind. So, keep that in mind, it will become more important as we continue diving into this mind model. Now we will start with the conscious mind first and work our way into the subconscious mind.

The conscious mind is the part of us that we are aware of. It is the part that we are using to think about thoughts right now, such as where you're sitting while you're reading this book, what clothes you're wearing, the tasks you must do, such as grocery shopping and feeding the dog.

It is also the part of awareness of the room or building that you are currently sitting in. Your conscious mind is also the rational and analytical part. It's responsible for the thinking and judging that occurs in your mind.

If you know anything about the Star Trek series that was on TV, your conscious mind is represented best by the character Spock. As you begin to describe his character it's obvious of his incredible decision-making power.

He can offer extremely logical explanations for everything that is often the line he uses determining if something is logical or not. Yet despite this deep and impressive analytical ability as you begin to watch a few episodes you become aware that Spock was missing something much more important than any logical intellectual ability.

His character was missing of vital asset: heart.

You see one thing Spock did not have and was trained not to ever express was emotions. Just like the conscious mind doesn't, Spock had no emotions.

Now looking at the mind model and how it works we need to understand that rationality is a key important part of the mind in the way *humans must have a reason for everything*. Let me say that again, humans must have a reason and a rationale for everything even if that rationale is <u>completely inaccurate</u>.

It's for this reason that I call the conscious mind, *the lying rational mind.*

Lying?

Yes, because remember it is the weakest, the least informed, last to know part of us, yet it speaks the loudest, is responsible for generating the voice that we hear, and is very convincing at times and yet is completely inaccurate of what the deep underlying truths are.

Said another way, our ability to rationalize the actions that we do is what contributes to keeping us sane. This also makes it apparent that to solve our problems, such as reversing anxiety and panic disorders, it cannot be achieved using our conscious mind because it is not capable of viewing anything besides *itself.* It is convinced that it is in charge.

Let's explore the question of what is the underlying mechanism that is responsible for putting a person into a mental institution.

Several people may say it's a matter of whether a person is dangerous to himself or others, yet that's not it at all. Mental institutions can harbor some of the gentlest, the kindest and most harmless people you may ever meet while there are some quite dangerous people who are walking the streets right now. Some of these dangerous are in control of even bigger agendas, but that is another discussion entirely.

The answer to this question isn't a person's ability to rationalize his or her actions. Nearly all professional measures will always view a person to be sane *if they can rationalize their actions* no matter how inaccurate false or misaligned, they are with universal truths.

For example, a person who smokes cigarettes can do so peacefully and with a sense that they are justified in doing it just as long as they are able to rationalize this action. I once heard that to rationalize something means to make it into a "rational lie" and that definition absolutely fits this description.

A cigarette smoker or a person who vapes may indicate that they do so because it is relaxing, calms their nerves and maybe even helps the person with stress and increases their focus.

So, is this a true statement? The truth is smoke can increase both the heart rate and blood pressure and even increase hand tremors up to 300 percent! How can this possibly relax them, calm their nerves, and do anything of the sort with helping with stress?

In reality holding, a cigarette requires using a hand and the action of using a hand requires constant attention as the hands take up a tremendous amount of bandwidth and real estate on the surface of the brain.

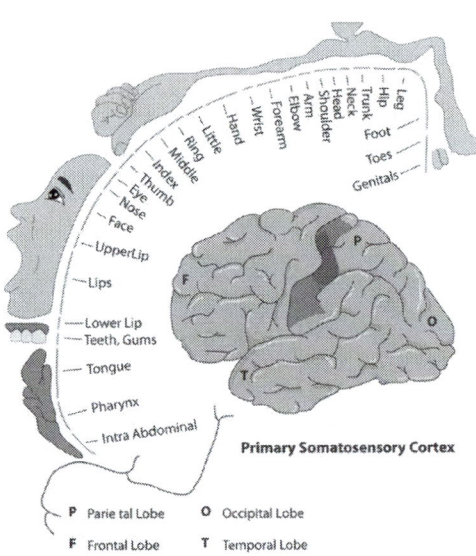

The Effect of Limb Amputation on the Somatosensory Homunculus

Primary Somatosensory Cortex

P Parietal Lobe   O Occipital Lobe
F Frontal Lobe   T Temporal Lobe

Looking at this view of a homunculus shows how much neurological circuitry goes into operating our hands alone and *this will be of utmost importance* as we go into the techniques later.

The point is the constant requirement and neurological attention of holding a cigarette consumes 30 or more percent of conscious resources of the brain during the act of a person smoking a cigarette. So, this can do nothing more physically than distract us and make us momentarily diverted while smoking or vaping.

However, as long as a rational lying mind can fabricate a reason for the action, the person remains to have some level of peace. This again is why we call the conscious mind the lying rational mind.

The minds rationalizing faculties require no alignment with universal truth.

Legendary Psychologist Mihaly Csikszentmihalyi pointed out that the conscious mind is aware of around *126 bits per second* of information while the subconscious mind processes *2.3 million bits per second* which mathematically equates to the conscious mind being .006% and the subconscious mind being 99.994% of our overall mind.

Now you can see why the conscious mind is the least informed last to know part of us and that .006% is the part of us that generates the voice in our head that we hear and is so convincing to us on why we do the things we do.

Understanding this, it's easy to see why most people with chaos in their lives or their health *consciously* believe that everything is just fine, while the vehicle of their life is going 100 miles an hour, in the wrong direction on a one-way street, smashing into the guardrails and street signs all the while the conscious mind is saying to the person, "Everything is going just fine!"

Understanding your mind is a rational lying mind will prepare you for success as we go deeper into these techniques later in the book.

Clinically I see this every day. A person comes to me, and they are distraught about a recent breakup, or a divorce and they are convincingly telling themself that their current problems in their life are all due to their previous spouse. I listen patiently and compassionately and then when we begin working together, I ask the only source that knows, which would be their subconscious (not the conscious mind).

Suddenly this person regresses to an age between 0 to five years old of where the first initial event was planted like a seed put in fertile soil, and this "problem" had absolutely nothing to do with their divorce and their former spouse. Yet their conscious lying rational mind convinced them otherwise. When we solve it there, in that moment, suddenly their former spouse no longer bothers them at all, to their utter astonishment!

Another trait of our lying rational and analytical mind is also where we originate our willpower from.

You may have been taught throughout your life to change your habits simply by mustering up enough willpower. This is usually the case every year with New Year's resolutions. As you can guess many of those habits are unsuccessfully changed. Why?

The first clue that willpower is inadequate to affect any habit or internal change is that willpower is part of the conscious mind and remember the conscious mind is the weakest, least informed, last to know part of us.

Willpower cannot change habits because it's not part of the inner subconscious mind! There is a common phrase that emphasizes this more and it goes something like, "when will and imagination meet, imagination always wins."

Imagine for a moment you layout a long 2 x 4 piece of lumber on the ground and practice walking across it always keeping your feet completely on the board. When you're walking across the board and it's laying on the grass covered ground, walking across this board seems like a pretty simple task, right?

Take this same 2 x 4 board and put it between two skyscrapers when the ground is a great distance below and suddenly walking across this board becomes a very daunting overwhelming task that may even put a person into a state of panic. How does this happen?

Because imagination is part of the very powerful inner Subconscious mind and willpower is part of the weak conscious mind.

When a person heals, it is never a matter of this individual winning some battle of inner voices by mustering tremendous willpower. Far from it. Permanent and dramatic healing can only be achieved by shifting and changing old perceptions that are stored within the goal achieving subconscious mind. After this occurs, they resonate in complete harmony with a newfound conscious intent. Mustering willpower is not the answer that many of us have been led to believe it is.

The next part of the conscious mind that we will discuss is memory capacity. The conscious mind is temporary memory only having a weak and very finite amount. The subconscious mind in contrast has an infinite unlimited capacity of permanent memory and this memory all begins at the moment of conception, not birth.

Now in terms of memory, I just mentioned a generalized statement that memory begins at the moment of conception and yet there is something else that we should briefly address. It has been ignored by modern medicine for a long time until more recently and some small, isolated groups of scientists and researchers are accepting it and assisting to make more sense of it.

This is the concept of cellular memory. Simply put, it's the idea that the brain doesn't contain memories any more than a radio contains the band members within it that are responsible for generating the music we hear. The brain is compared to a transistor in a radio as music doesn't come from the radio. It comes through the radio. Thought doesn't come *from* the brain. It comes *through* the brain.

Adding to this are the cases of fascinating reports in hundreds of organ recipients. They have reported disturbing experiences after having an organ transplanted that indicates that cellular memories are passed from donor to recipient.

Clinically, I have witnessed this. I had a patient who suddenly had food cravings shift to something they never cared to eat before. After a kidney transplant, she began finding herself craving McDonalds' French fries. She inquired a little deeper and found that her donor's favorite snack food was McDonald's fries.

A collaboration of these kinds of cases are nothing new either. In 2005, a woman in France is haunted by vivid images of her donor's death in a car crash. Furthermore, in 2006 a man living in Croatia develops an obsession for domestic chores after receiving a kidney from a deceased housewife. More bizarre and startling incidents have also been noted. In 2007, Georgia, USA a man given the heart of a suicide victim kills himself in exactly the same way of his donor (7).

A Professor of neurology Dr. Gary Schwartz has been researching this phenomenon for the past 15 years. He says, "There are now enough of those cases available to justify saying this is a serious possibility." Dr Schwartz is the co-author of a paper that analyzes 10 real life case histories in which transplant patients claim they have acquired personality traits from their donors.

The reason that I mention this in this book is because when I do regression work, and we begin to utilize some of the techniques later detailed in this book, it is important to realize that on occasion, the traumas, or imprinted experiences from memories that we carry which influence us and our behaviors *may not be of ours in origin.* (7)

Although our most powerful and influential experiences are from our childhood, we need to be open to the possibility and flexible when we discuss topics such as the origin of memories.

When a person usually of an older age say that they have a poor memory I want to point out that this is actually a very incorrect statement. The fact is that they have an excellent permanent memory, and they are just referring to the wrong one and there's a very good reason for that.

If a person cannot easily access his subconscious mind where the permanent memory is stored it's because of a *very important apparatus is standing in the way*. In fact, this apparatus is the most important part of the conscious mind it has everything to do with internal change and because of this importance we will introduce it later.

Now, let's go back to the conscious mind and briefly discuss the last trait of it we will cover. The conscious mind is a very weak mind when compared to the subconscious mind's power.

Let's put it this way, if the conscious mind or the part of you that you are aware of that was the power of an automobile engine, the subconscious mind in contrast has the power of the Milky Way Galaxy.

Now, let's dive into and introduce the powerful force referred to as the Subconscious Mind. Illustrated as the much bigger and lower centered circle in the graphic, it is this that has been described as "the power that does the work" as its limitations are unknown.

Now, before we get into an inventory of characteristics of the subconscious mind, I want to point out two very important characteristics of the subconscious mind.

The first in contrast to the conscious mine's weakness, the subconscious mind is **the single most powerful goal achieving agency known to man**. From the beginning of recorded time man has known that it exists.

As we have already briefly explored, the mind goes beyond the brain and body in numerous ways. Combine this with the goal achieving capabilities the subconscious mind harbors and this combination is nothing short of miraculous.

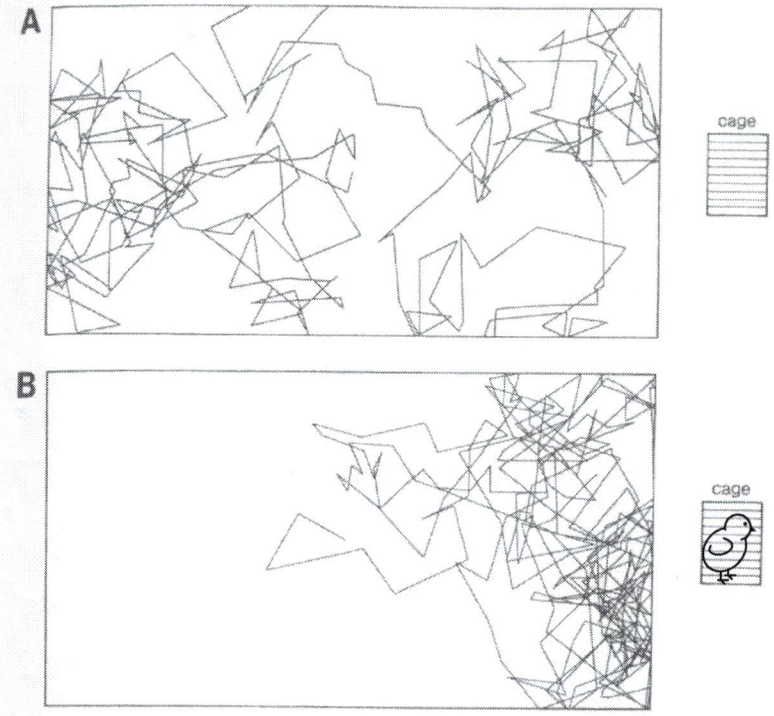

Figure 16.1 The path traced out by the moving robot in experiments of René Peoc'h. A: A control experiment in which the cage was empty. B: An experiment in which day-old chicks imprinted on the robot were kept in the cage. (Reproduction courtesy of René Peoc'h)

Take the example of Ren'e Peoc'h, Phd and his experiments he and his team of scientist conducted with day old chickens. Dr Peoc'h and his team used a special mechanized robot that was designed specifically to move around randomly in a small, controlled arena.

The robot would move around without specific directions, 50% of the time moving left and 50% of the time moving right and with his team he tracked the movements that this mechanized robot performed in the arena. As you can imagine over a period of time, the robot covered the entire arena equally moving around in specific random movements which they tracked. This path represents the top graph labeled A.

The next thing Dr. Poec'h introduced was one-day old chicks in the same arena as the robot. It is well known that day-old chickens and day-old ducklings imprint an emotional bond on the first object they see moving, as if it was their mother. It doesn't matter if it's a dog running by, a child riding a bicycle, or something else moving--the day-old chicken and/or day-old ducklings will automatically assume that it's their mother, form an emotional bond with it and begin to follow it.

As a result, these day-old chicks began to follow the robot as it moved around randomly. Overtime after the chicks had emotionally bonded to the robot, he removed them from the arena and put them in a container which allowed them to see the robot but no longer follow it or get near it.

What followed is absolutely shocking. It is a clear demonstration of the power of mind extending beyond the brain (in this case the brain of a chicken) and the power of the goal achieving subconscious as it influenced the robot's movement no longer a random pattern, but instead it remained in the arena location near the baby chick. This second pattern is represented by graph label B.

Looking at this figure shows more than the before and after of the experiment: this is a direct map of you and your truest nature. This is of course, beyond the range of what the physical senses can detect. To summarize this nature, let's observe the quote form Wallace Wattles' book *The Science of Getting Rich* in which he states:

"There is a thinking stuff from which all things are made, and which, in its original state, permeates penetrates and fills the interspaces of the universe.

A thought, in this substance produces the thing that is imagined by the thought.

Man can form things in his thought, and by impressing his thought upon Formless Substance, can cause the thing he thinks about to be created."

The thinking stuff in which he refers to in this moment of course is what we have come to know as the quantum field, which is an infinite field completely composed of frequencies that carry pliable information with an unlimited amount of energy vibrating beyond the physical world that we know and experience with our five senses.

Quantum physics is the most valid of all science today[9] and it is within this quantum field in which all possibilities and probabilities exist.

Imagine the quantum field being equivalent to a Wi-Fi Internet field.

Now for a moment realize that whatever appears on screen of the computer is dictated by what part of the internet that is retrieved. Whatever we look up on the search engine will determine what pops up on the computer screen. This is an easy concept for most people to understand.

Now, compare this computer screen to every part of our life. The part of the quantum field, (which has unlimited possibilities available to us), that we access and manifest into our personal experiences, dictates what appears on the "screen" of our lives as our individual experiences.

When a person lives their life within the restrictions of unhealed trauma, such as PTSD, they are interacting within a narrow bandwidth of the available information and frequencies of quantum possibilities and probabilities.

The more severe the trauma a person endures, the narrower the band of frequency they are operating within.

The perception this person has is constricted and therefore the potential they have to intentionally manifest positive achievements is limited. Once a person has expanded their self-identity, and their consciousness expands, their sense of the possible also expands. It is here where your healing awaits. It is here where the relationship you desire, dream vacation or the abundance you want for your family resides.

As we will soon visit in more details, consider the researchers who began studying the subatomic world and found that everything in our physical universe is made-up of a nucleus surrounded by an enormous field containing electrons, known as atoms.

When closer examining this field, they discovered that it's so massive in contrast to the difference between the tiny electrons and the "space" surrounding the nucleus. Yet this space is far from void and actually composed of an infinite level of energetic frequencies that makeup an interconnected limitless field of information.

It is within this field of information they found that the electrons seem to operate by a completely different set of laws and behaviors then our larger more tangible universe. This is because the electron exist within infinite behavioral patterns and these behavioral patterns becomes apparent when an observer focuses their attention on any given choice of a specific idea.

Said another way, whatever idea an individual thinks about with emotion, is impressed into this Formless Substance and begins the process of that idea coming into the physical manifestation, just like a computer screen displaying whatever is searched out from the internet field.

More on this later, but for now, recognize that if the observer focuses their attention somewhere else, the subatomic particle dissolves back into the infinite field as energy.

Therefore, it's important to recognize that your *thoughts are things that affect other things* and if you are wanting to change your life in some way it's important to recognize that things are never brought into existence or experiences by focusing on their opposite.

Recall earlier, I mentioned that a person who experiences trauma has a tendency to always see the worst-case scenarios in life's circumstances. You must realize first, that before we go through the process of clearing past traumatic imprints, we need to understand that we need to also condition ourselves for looking for the good things in life. To accept who we are and forgive our past experiences. We need to know that our thoughts are incredibly powerful and to not have a mindful understanding of how we direct our thoughts, and our emotions will make our efforts to change and heal all be of no use.

In other words, a person never becomes wealthy by contemplating and studying poverty. Health is never obtained by studying disease and contemplating on illness. Righteousness is never achieved by an individual who constantly studies sin and you will never be free from suffering by listening to, thinking about, and having intense feelings towards all the fearful, unfortunate bad things that could happen.

It is far more important to focus on what you do want and what it is you are looking to achieve. Learn to screen every thought you come across and every idea that pops in your head and ask yourself is this an idea taking me in the direction towards my goal I want to achieve? Is this worth getting emotionally involved in?

As you begin to gain response flexibility, this is one of the most powerful questions that you use to screen ideas either helping you or hindering you. This is where it starts. This is where the awareness begins. It starts here and it starts with understanding that if you are not happy with the results in your life, in your health, in your wealth and/or your overall emotional state, it starts by understanding that *you are emotionally involved and some kind of negative destructive idea.*

You may have not put it there, but you can change it by recognizing this.
What happened to you is not your fault. Your childhood traumas that have occurred to you happened at a time when you were too young to defend yourself and too vulnerable to know what was happening to you. You could not reject the environmental information around your earliest years any more than a mirror can reflect something else besides what is in placed front of it.

You live your life, you solve your problems, you choose your relationships, you heal your body, and you choose your politics all based upon the way you think and the way feel about yourself. (Like it or not) Remember, don't let your conscious rational lying brain get the best of you!

However, up until this point you may have never known that you create your destiny. From this point forward, break the cycle by watching, screening, and observing anything and everything that you allow yourself to get emotionally involved in or have intense feelings towards. If it is destructive, I guarantee you it will only lead to more destruction.

The subconscious mind is the emotional mind, and whatever goes into the subconscious mind instantly changes the vibrational signature in every atom in your body and within your life experiences. It has been said that what has happened to you is not your fault, *but it is your responsibility to do something about it*. If you do not know where to start, it starts with never allowing yourself to become emotionally involved with any idea, concept or subject that is taking you in the direction of destruction. This is where it starts.

We are the only form of life with the ability to consciously self-regulate our biology on demand. We are also the only form of life on the planet that gives significant emotional meaning to our lives. (10)

Your neurology is the single largest organic antenna on the planet. It is constantly emitting a vibrational signature out to the universe that is the composite and the sum total of every filter and program running in your body right now.

It is the sum of every feeling you have both on a conscious and subconscious level. That's what you're sending out to the universe. If you purify the signal, clean up the rubbish, decide where and what you focus your emotional attention on, what you want will manifest cleaner, more purely and much faster because the bandwidth of your cosmic internet expands.

Everything that vibrates, from the electron to the Milky Way Galaxy behaves this way.

Ever heard of the McClintock effect? Published in the journal Nature in 1971, Martha McClintock investigated the menstrual cycle synchronizations which takes place when two or more women become in more proximal range to each other. (11)

How does this occur? As we just learned, your physical body is composed of atoms, and they are constantly vibrating.

What your atoms do and the harmony or disharmony at which they vibrate, is what your biology functions at. The harmony or disharmony that your biological processes function at is how well your physiology functions.

How harmonic or disharmonic your physiology vibrates at is how well your cognition functions. It is this phenomenon responsible for why you feel more comfortable around people who have the same ethnic background as you. That's also why you feel more comfortable with people that are the same gender as you. That's why you feel more comfortable around people who share the same interests, such as sports, religious affiliations, or political stances as you.

It's the structure and the patterns below the surface that are the truth. Everything else that is interpreted by our five senses is the illusion.

The second characteristic of the subconscious mind is that **it cannot judge a single suggestion placed within it.**

Judgement is purely a conscious mind function, and the subconscious mind is incapable of judging or considering any idea placed into it. It is similar to a fertile plot of soil that will grow anything that's planted in it, with no questions asked. Poison ivy or roses, the soil makes no distinction as to whatever is grown in it.

This is such an important point that it should be repeated. The *single most powerful relentless goal achieving agency known to man is incapable of judging a single suggestion.*

Genevieve Behrend, a pupil to the phenomenal author and mental scientist Thomas Troward, confirms these statements in her book *Your Invisible Power.*

All space is filled with a creative power, as we just learned about within the contents of the atom. This creative power is amenable to suggestion meaning that its entire nature is *responsiveness.*

Lastly, it can only work by deductive methods. This means it is has no ability to judge or change any suggestion placed into it any more than a mirror can reflect something back other than the object placed in front of it. (Yes you read that again)

This is the unseen part of us is constantly at work, molding our thoughts feelings and actions in a way that are below our conscious awareness. The subconscious mind has been referred to by numerous names including the heart by the Greeks while others called it the soul. Some call it the Super Ego, the inner power, the Super consciousness, the unconscious, the subconscious, and a variety of other names.

As we touched on, it isn't to be confused with an organ or so-called physical matter such as the brain or heart. Ancient philosophers often referred to it as the spirit. Dr Joseph Murphy indicated that it is a part of the supreme intelligence to which we are all linked, and it is recognized as the essence of life.

It acts similar to a warning sensation alerting us in times of lingering trouble, which explains the case of our "gut feelings" warning us of impending danger, and often it aids us in what seems impossible. It seeks to guide us in many ways and when properly engaged performs so-called supernatural events, as we just saw with the baby chicks influencing the behaviors of a mechanized robot.

Now let's take a brief inventory of the characteristics within the subconscious mind.

The subconscious mind is where we harbor our imagination and contrary to what some people may understand, imagination is much more than just creativity. Imagination is, in many ways, one of several perceptual filters that gives us our view of the world we live in. Everyone's imagination is either working *with them* or *against them*.

This is because we all have a perception of the world that is as unique as each individual fingerprint. Even though a person's perception has nothing to do with universal laws or divine order, to that person, their perception is what they view is absolute truth.

To understand this more let's take two people off the street, stand them beside each other and examine each one's individual perception. To one of those people, they may view the world has been completely overpopulated, with not near enough food to feed everyone, ecology is diminished, climate change is going to do us all in, there's a new variant in the air and all the money that exists is in the hands of a very few at the top of the world which is about to end.

Now we've all met these people. Some of them may be close to us or our relatives and no matter what you tell them or what they hear, they're convinced of upcoming doom and gloom.

Now let's look at the other individual who has a personal vision and a specific goal in mind, have put in several years of hard work making this a reality, knows where they're going, knows exactly what they want, has finally received the financial means to make it happen and is ready to cut the ribbon on the new family business. This individual perceives the world as looking bright and holding infinite opportunity.

Now the point is that the world has not changed a bit, but only to what each person sees is real. So, imagination is our perception of the world around us, how we view ourselves, how we view life and how we interpret the experiences we have, whether good or bad. Imagination has nothing to do with universal truth. It is simply a perception.

What's important to understand is for each individual, once a perception is imprinted at the deepest levels of the subconscious mind in our earliest years of life-- good or bad, positive or negative--the single most powerful goal achieving agency known to man and accepts it as fact, it will set out to turn make it so!

It would be wise to understand this part of yourself, to gain rapport with it and work with it if you were to improve any area in your life. In fact, don't expect any area of your life to improve if you choose to ignore the power of your subconscious mind because doing so is equivalent to ignoring a garden with fertile soil and just allowing the weeds to quickly take it over.

Imagination is our perception of the world around us and we are part of that world and not only are we a part of it, we are a participant in it, not an observer as John Archibald Wheeler so accurately stated.

This is also how we define the commonly used and perhaps overly franchised term self-image.

The building blocks of our self-image are solidified between the moment of conception to around the age of five years old. Likewise, this perception has nothing to do with the realities of our truest potential; it's just a perception based off our earliest childhood experiences.

The subconscious mind works to achieve manifestations under the guidance and perhaps limitations of whatever's in harmony with the self-image and nothing beyond it. In other words, if you have the idea and feelings operating within your self-image that you don't deserve "X" or you don't deserve "Y", even if you win the lottery or receive a large inheritance from a relative, you will always find a way to sabotage yourself.

As you can imagine this is what happens to a great significant majority of the people who win the lottery and why they are bankrupt within five years. The same thing happens to pro athletes, as nearly 80 percent of them are completely bankrupt three years after their retirement (12).

Jim Rohn said it best: "If someone gives you $1,000,000 you best become a millionaire quickly, so you get to keep the money. Otherwise soon enough it will all disappear." This statement demonstrates how the self-image limits one in terms of prosperity. It also demonstrates how your self-image determines the bandwidth of infinite possibilities and probabilities within the quantum world that you have access to.

Without expanding the bandwidth by clearing out your past traumas, and observing where you focus your emotional attention, do not expect anything to permanently change.

As you can begin to see, the self-image is not just limited to the topic of prosperity and financial abundance. The self-image is also the governing vessel in terms of personalities traits characteristics and all things relating to the health of the individual as well.

For example, in our functional medicine clinic we helped dozens of people completely reverse the effects, the symptoms, and all the clinical evidence including blood sugar levels that are associated with diabetes type 2. We taught them how to eat correctly, about incorporating nutritional support for their bodies, the importance of physical activity, mindfulness exercises like breathing and meditation and yet time and time again we could not keep a majority of them from going back to their old ways that manifested diabetes type 2 in the first place.

This was simply because their self-image matched a "diabetic" and did not match a healthy relaxed person with stable blood sugar levels. It was only after we started working with the person self-image that we noticed the person stayed healthier long term and years later are still completely symptom free. They learned to see the best parts of life and it reflected the best back to them.

Here's how the self-image governs a person's life: I can instantly make a connection with a person who has been called and labeled as clumsy simply by asking the person if they've ever heard something like: "Correct me if I'm wrong but you've probably heard this on multiple occasions. 'Oh my goodness!! It looked like you stumbled on purpose!' "

Now this person who has identified himself as clumsy will respond, "How did you know that?"

The answer lies and fully understanding how the mind model works.

The subconscious mind is the single most powerful goal achieving agency known to humanity and once the label of *clumsy* is programmed into this part of the inner mind, the subconscious mind without judging or analyzing this decision---immediately moves this into form.

Now the individual may grow tired of having such a label and will naturally try to control their behavior by steering clear of table tops, breakables, like glasses desk, corners, curbs and table legs under the assumption (from the lying rational brain) that everything will calm down, the person begins to move more efficiently and the disasters of being clumsy we'll come to an end.

This is also where they are completely wrong.

The subconscious mind epitomizes tenacity and relentless dedication to put whatever is in it, into reality.

Even when a person who has a self-image of being clumsy does everything possible, they can steer clear of disaster by keeping distance from objects that are breakable. The subconscious mind is forced to go out of its way to achieve that goal of clumsiness. When this subliminal creative stretch takes place in the achievement of clumsiness, anyone witnessing this is under the impression that the person who just performed the clumsy behavior did so on purpose. **It's important to point out that the person's conscious mind would have no idea what the witness was talking about when asked about it.**

All your personas and your identities are simply beliefs and behaviors that you've become used to. They are what is familiar and comfortable. However, that does not mean you do not have anything else, nor does it mean you cannot become anything else.

Every single person that's alive on earth right now as well as yourself holds a series of perceptions about yourself including what you are worth and what you deserve in life.
For people with chronic illness, autoimmune conditions, and other terminal labeled diseases, they carry a deep perception of how much punishment and hardship is called for.

It's important to point out that when we discuss the goal achieving mind doing its job and what these inner perceptions held in the subconscious mind are brought to achieve have absolutely nothing to do with what the person *consciously* says that he or she desires.

In fact, it may be that some of these people say they desire healing, health and wellness but there is something much deeper happening that we will discuss soon.

As well as the imaginative and the perceptive part of our mind, the subconscious mind is also where our permanent memory is stored.

Think of every grain of data that you have ever encountered through your five senses all the way back to the time within the womb up until the present moment, it is stored in the subconscious mind and available for recall and review. This is the part of us that you could point out that makes us who we really are.

Without your awareness or consent you will think your next thought, act your next action, and feel your next feeling based upon everything that has ever happened before in your past. One of my mentors said that we do not think.

We only remember.

What we think we are thinking is simply remembering, correlating, comparing, and analyzing everything that's ever happened to us before, to what is happening right now in the present moment.

In fact, this next statement is incredibly accurate and will become very relevant as we continue our journey through this book and these techniques. *We are the sum total of all of our past events* with the events from the age of conception to age five being the most powerful and the most influential.

The next thing about our subconscious mind that we should really understand is that it's also the emotional mind. Now, by emotional mind, I mean *all emotions* including all the good ones and the not so good ones.

The word emotion refers to energy in motion, so it is this energy that must be understood. Emotions correctly guided, can improve your life in numerous ways. We as human beings are emotional creatures, and it is important that they all have a purpose and are very powerful. They also must be understood for your life to change. Emotions are so powerful they can go either way on you. Emotions can either build or destroy so you really must employ emotions correctly.

Emotions have this ability because they are literally energy in motion. Previously we looked at Dr Renee Peoc'h's experiments involving baby chicks ability to influence the behavior of a mechanized robot by employing emotion bonding with it. It was the *emotional bond* between the day-old chicken and the robot which influenced the change and behavior of the robot.

It is the subconscious mind that controls the vibrational state of the body, and it does this through the emotional state. Whatever idea a person (or animal) is emotionally involved with is ultimately what controls the vibration of the atoms within their body.

We have 50 trillion cells that make up our physical body and each individual cell is made-up of 100 trillion atoms.

Imagine a couple arguing over something. Now imagine seeing a person laughing hysterically while enjoying a show at a comedy club. Now imagine a woman crying while watching a sad scene in a dramatic movie. What is common in each of these images is that they are emotionally involved in what they are observing, the idea passes into the subconscious mind and is manifested as a vibratory state we call emotions.

Each one of these examples of a person is in a different state, and their atoms of their bodies are varying at completely different frequencies.

In a decade of work as a doctor with patients from across the globe with every variance of range of symptoms you could imagine from multiple sclerosis to Lyme disease, digestive disorders of every kind to chronic pain, the one thing that's very clear amongst every one of them was *their emotional state was in disharmony.*

They had intense feelings towards something destructive in their life, most often originating from unresolved trauma that was constantly playing a cyclic emotional cascade of events, and this led to their body being in a very poor vibration.

This means in all my clinical findings there's one thing that is clear: *there's no such thing as a person with any chronic illness or autoimmune condition or malignancy of any kind who is emotionally healthy.*

Said another way, wherever you look closer at a chronically ill person, you'll find they have intense feelings of some kind towards a destructive idea. The ideas that are the most commonly associated with chronic diseases in the body are *criticism* (of self or others), *anger, resentment* and *guilt.* (13)

The ideas that allow healing to occur within our body are *love* (which means only seeing the best in everything and everyone, including yourself) and *forgiveness*, as these bring harmony into the subconscious mind and ultimately harmony within the body's vibration.

Knowing this, it is a wise choice to begin observing your thoughts and monitoring what you allow yourself to develop intense feelings towards. It is something I drill to every one of my patients to memorize, as it doesn't matter how clean their diet is, how much they exercise or what kind of spring water they drink, if they are emotionally involved in a destructive idea, their body will reflect this and originate some form of dis-ease.

One of the things that we should be aware of within our society is that we give free ring to filth in the reflection of obscene language, sex and violence and a majority of the TV shows. And we do this under the banner of free speech.

All this takes place while any grain of goodness must fight for its right to even whisper. One reason for this is something called *consumer science*. These are a group of scientists that are all too familiar with the mind model and they understand consumption as well as determining what you get to see and hear through your TV, radio, social media networks, broadcasts, and all means of printed media.

You see, consumer scientists have figured out that people will consume without reason when they are feeling empty. Contrast this to whenever people feel good and they fell whole, this breed's fullness into the subconscious and these people don't consume without reason.

Filth, vulgarity and conflict breeds bigotry violence and corruption.

Now consumer scientists work with another group that I will call *equalologists*. Equalologist are those who campaign for laws designed to scare us into not feeling the emotions that were hypnotically installed by the consumer scientists through our television and media.

Now, let's briefly discuss hypnosis and what it technically means. **Hypnosis** *is the bypass of the critical faculty of the conscious mind and the establishment of acceptable selective thinking.*

Now if you contemplate this definition for a moment, you will come to the realizations that there is not much that you encounter that doesn't accomplish this. Although we will go into more details on this soon, let's briefly look at what utilizes hypnotic principles more then we might be aware of.

Movies accomplish this as *actors are the best hypnotist in the world*. They can take you out of your world and suck you right into theirs. They set up conditions in your mind that tickle your emotions and imagination (traits of the subconscious) which were different before watching the movie and suddenly you find yourself following the context of whatever the producer or the director or the station wants you to have, *all while your conscious mind is not aware of it.*

If you desire to be in a terrible state of vibration, just watch the unending variety of violent TV shows available along with the media. A state of chaos, uncertainty and impending doom will be delivered right on time. With that, the feeling of anxiety and helplessness will soon follow.

Books are capable of this as well, as this is the intention of this one. (Grin) Think about the hypnosis definition again and you'll see that advertising does this as well. Why do you think all, but a few countries ban direct to consumer commercials advertising drugs using attractive men and women actors? Ever watch a drug commercial?

United States television advertisements are flooded with these very commercials always linking a medication to an answer in a *hypnotic medium* to bypass your thinking mind and establish selective thinking.

There is not much that does not have the capacity to bypass your critical faculty and direct your thoughts in a certain direction, many times without your awareness, in a certain and specific ways.

For example, religions have stock and trade of accomplishing this feat. Every single preacher is a hypnotist by, using emotion, tells you about the glories of heaven and the fires of hell, they get your emotional part of your brain active, known as the limbic system, and anything with great emotion passes right by the critical faculty and without knowing it or having any awareness of it, you suddenly become hyper suggestible.

It certainly doesn't stop there.
There is a secret government that Sigmund Freud's nephew Edward Bernays wrote about. He's also the founder and father of public relations, propaganda and he coined the term the *engineering of consent* that was published in 1947.

The secret government I was referring to is the media; they run the entire planet simply by telling you what to think, what to believe, what is true and what is false — all without your awareness or consent. This is also why there is such a close relationship between governments and media.

Edward Bernays is also responsible for giving millions of women cancer because he convinced them to start smoking.

Detailed in his essay, accounts the story of George Washington Hill who was president of the American Tobacco company, and he hired Edward Bernays in 1928 to lead a campaign to entice women to smoke cigarettes as the campaign hypnotically induced them to change their attitudes from a social taboo to a more socially acceptable act.

Bernays accomplished this by associating women's' smoking with the idea of power and freedom and he used the slogan Torches of Freedom during a famous parade in New York City. (14) He convinced them that by smoking you could be a woman and match the power level as a man. This strategy led to millions of women all over the world to begin smoking after World War 2.

The point is that by allowing negative emotions to be hypnotically installed by our consumer scientist and then punishing those unknowing subjects if they act out the post hypnotic suggestions installed by these creators of emptiness is very deadly to the human psyche.

Holding in negative emotions is *repression* and repressed emotion is what breeds disease. Repressing emotion is also what fills prisons, kills people through chronic illness and it works right in conjunction with selling tremendous amounts of drugs and medicine.

The last thing that we will discuss regarding the subconscious mind is that it's a protective mind. It will protect us from dangers whether they are real or whether they're completely imagined. The subconscious mind interprets these threats as real, solid objects which is where phobias originate from, as well as periodic episodes of panic. A panic attack is when the subconscious mind is telling a person to get out of the current situation that it perceives as a danger.

Now as far as the protective mind goes, we must ask a few key questions: What's important to this mind? What are its priorities? What is it protecting and how? Well, this is relevant whenever we look at the basic essentials for every human being, the first one being security.

The second necessity would be connectedness, or what we could call "love". I put love in quotes because it is very important that we define exactly what this word means before moving on. **Love** means I *only see the best in you*, I welcome you in my presence, and I'm filled with joy to have you in my presence.

Now love is not less important than security however *security is the one thing that we as humans are all given a sample of by default.* This happens when we are in the womb which happens to be a warm safe secure environment we know as a human being.

It's the first thing we know for nine months while developing as a human being, before the sudden squeeze, a push, bright lights, a cold steel table and then we transition from the only environment we've ever known for nine months, which is a cozy environment, to someplace new and opposite of everything we ever knew for those first nine months.

Now here's where many people, including professionals, may misunderstand this, and they mistakenly align security with pleasure. Security doesn't come from pleasure for the first nine months.

It comes from what's familiar for the first nine months.

Think about this for a moment. For nine months it was the same thing every day. From the first moment that our soul took on a physical body, that's all we knew. Most people want to spin the word security and pleasure together as one thread and weave that thread throughout the entire phase of maternity. However, security is *not* that which is pleasurable. Security is that which is familiar!

Let's examine this another way. Let's look at how we build perceptions.

The moment you acquire a perception you now have some bit of data to compare new additional data against.

From here this comparison will be extremely relevant to everything moving forward. Any new experience that harmonizes or is in synchronicity in any way with that first impression will create a very secure feeling within the body.

It's almost as if a deep-down sensation says to us "The rest of the world agrees with how I view this perception." This is a very comforting and secure feeling. When any new information or data coming from the outside perceived from our five senses and is not in harmony with this inner perception, it suddenly creates a very insecure feeling.

In a moment we will visit this mechanism known as a critical faculty that we have already touched on multiple times in much more in depth, as it is very important.

Love, or connectedness, may be just as important as security and the lack of it may be even more detrimental. The difference between love is that *we are not guaranteed a taste of this by default.* What do I mean by this?

If two love starved people get together and bring a child into this world, they cannot give that child what they themselves don't have. Just like the old saying says you cannot pour from an empty cup. In the same way you cannot give another person what you yourself don't first possess.

So, a child born of two love starved parents has never had the experience of tasting love. This child does not know what love feels like, looks like, or sounds like but the child does have something inside we might consider a calling. The child is looking for "it", but he or she doesn't know what that internal driving factor necessarily is. That driving factor is the *necessity of connectedness*.

Now this child accepts whatever is offered first in life as "love" and accepts it without comparison. If this perception of love is distance and criticism, well, distance and criticism become the subconscious mind's inner goal achieving definition of love.

As this child grows into an adult still seeking that love, that person's subconscious mind will naturally gravitate them towards people whose tendency and behavior are one of distance and criticism.

We've all heard of or have known people who "married their father or mother" or the people that date the same person with a different face. And now you understand a bit more about what drives this unconscious unintentional behavior.

It is not a conscious choice. Remember my story from the first chapter and how my childhood conditions drove me to act out certain behaviors all to reproduce those "familiar" feelings? These are all unconscious patterns.

Now let's talk about the very last and the most important piece of the conscious mind that we've motioned several times already. I referred to it earlier as the "barrier" that guards your subconscious mind. It is known as the **critical faculty**. You may have noticed I said "conscious mind" because it resides in the conscious mind, but it takes orders directly from the subconscious mind.

Your critical faculty has one purpose; it is designed to keep you from changing too fast. If you didn't have a critical faculty, anything you were told would go right into the powerful subconscious mind and have as much validity as anything else in your life, such as where you were born, your name and your date of birth.

This would cause you to be a constant Yo-Yo, getting kicked around like a football, buffeted, and constantly knocked off of course by any and all suggestions you ever hear or see. For this reason, your critical faculty has a setting on it; *it only lets in what's already there*. What was there already was installed between the years of conception and age five.

Remember the two things I pointed out about the subconscious mind; it's the most powerful goal achieving agency known to man and it cannot judge a single suggestion. Looking at this you'll notice that's a very vulnerable combination.

If any random suggestion reached the subconscious mind, it would accept that suggestion as fact and make it so with no questions asked!

Remember what we discussed and the paragraph on hypnosis? So, the critical faculty exists to protect this vulnerable nature of the subconscious mind and here's how it works.

It takes every incoming suggestion from the outside world and stops it in its tracks. It then compares that incoming suggestion to every perception that we hold on to that particular subject.

If the new suggestion is not in harmony with the previous older perception, the critical faculties main job--*that it does so incredibly effective*--is to stop the new suggestion and act as a mirror reflecting light and instantly reject it.

To emphasis this, let's read the quote put forth by Danish theologian and philosopher Soren Kierkegaard who said that the two ways to be fooled is to believe what *isn't* true, or secondly to *refuse* to believe what is true.

If the new suggestion is stopped in its tracks, analyzed and found to be in harmony or it matches the inner perceptions, the critical faculty swings wide open and allows it to pass right in.

It's at this moment that we encounter one of the most powerful laws of mind known as the *law of compounding*. The law of compounding states that every impression you ever perceive, no matter what it is, carries a specific weight, or a "mass of belief" you might say.

Every time a new suggestion from the outside world is stopped and found to be in harmony with our inner perception, just like an accumulating mass that grows larger and larger the weight of the new impression is added into the pre-existing belief, strengthening and reinforcing that perception.

It is through this compounding of thousands and thousands of experiences that our belief in that accumulating perception grows proportionately stronger and stronger overtime and over similar additional experiences.

This is the mechanism behind a person's subconscious goal achieving mind working to manifest perceptions with increasing or decreasing enthusiasm over time depending upon the individual's life accumulating experiences. These experiences factor either for or against the indexed weight of the first suggestion on any topic and any subject.

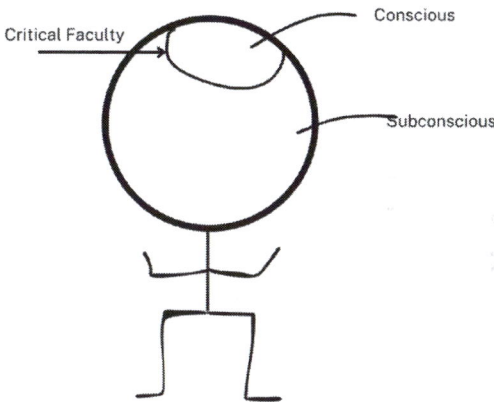

Take a moment and look at this figure. I believe it is an excellent example which sums up the role of the critical faculty, the job it does remarkably well along with the consequences of compounding events reinforcing beliefs, no matter how inaccurately portrayed or false they are, that we learn throughout our early life.

In the book The Republic, the ancient Greek philosopher Plato describes a chapter that was titled the Allegory of The Cave. Use your imagination and follow along in this illustration.

(15)

On one side of this picture, there is subterranean cave, and you see a group of prisoners who have been sequestered from birth to the confinements of this place. To them, the world they know is one of isolation, completely devoid of any contact with the outside world. They are bound by chains and restricted in their movements and can only perceive the inside of the cave walls their entire life.

As you can imagine, this makes them deprived of any ability to see or experience anything beyond their immediate environment. Behind them is an animatic fire that flickers and barely lights up their bland and dismal surroundings.

Occasionally, mysterious cloaked individuals walk behind the prisoners, and these unseen characters display various figures representing silhouettes of various animals, shapes, plants as well as a variety of other forms. As these silhouettes pass by the fire, their shadows portray elongated and distorted figures on the stone walls in the frontal view the prisoners.

Remember, these prisoners have no other experiences or history to go off of and this cave and these shadowy figures are all they know. This creates a "truth" for them in which they mistakenly assume these dancing illusions for their reality.

Now, imagine that one of these prisoners' shackles are removed and he is able to climb and escape the confinements of the cave, being newly exposed to a whole new world beyond the cave for the very first time.

The moment the sunlight hits his face, the intense brilliance of it initially hurts his eyes and the unfamiliar territory bewilders him to the core.

As he settles and locates a place to sit quietly with his thoughts, a deep-down awareness comes to the surface as he is confronted with the fact that his former perception of reality was merely a distorted illusion.

He feels a deep unpleasant shift now that he perceives the things that he observes all around him are in fact, real objects of an entirely different world then he has known. He begins to suffer as his previous reality is now in the process of being deconstructed before his very eyes.

This is a reminder of another law of mind that states that once a mind opens and is stretched to a new idea, it never returns to its original size.

As more time progresses, his eyes slowly adapt to the overwhelming brightness and his suffering slowly passes as he gets accustomed to his new perception. He begins perceiving the surface of shimmering bodies of water and observing the birds fly across the sky and the ever-shifting shapes of clouds above him.

Encouraged by his newfound recognition of what the world *actually* is, imagine the prisoner making his way back into the cave entrance with plans to share his divulgence with the other prisoners.

However, having grown accustomed to the bright sunlight, he now finds the darkness within the cave disorienting. As he finds the still shackled prisoners against the wall watching the shadows, he suddenly finds an unexpected struggle to discredit the wall displays and explain that these "aren't real" and "are just an illusion".

The other prisoners misconstruing his confusion, deduce that his experience into the outer world has left him *deranged, imbecilic* and *absurd*, thereby rejecting his attempts to liberate them. *It is the prisoner's critical faculty of their mind at work.*

Plato presents this metaphor as a representation of the predicament of an individual tasked with enlightening the mainstream crowd. A cold unfortunate realization is observed that most people not only find solace in their ignorance but also display hostility towards those who confront or oppose their preconceived notions.

Now, compare Plato's metaphor to a child who comes new into this world; they have no information in their permanent memory of the subconscious. It's like a blank computer disk with incredible storage capacity yet no data. If there's no data in the subconscious mind, there's nothing to compare against so there can't be a critical faculty. But the first time we take a newborn and whisper something in his or her ear, now there's a perception.

Now the critical faculty forms a little splotch around that one idea. From this point forward, any new subject that is heard will be stopped, instantly compared. If it is in harmony, it's automatically accepted and compounded, and that belief grows stronger. Any idea that is out of harmony is automatically rejected.

So, the persons critical faculty forms in bits and splashes around each and every new perception that hits the mind with a new subject. Once there is some piece of thought on one particular subject, there's a critical faculty formed to protect that idea.

By the time a child turns 4, the critical faculty has formed a solid barrier around all perceptions of self. By 12, the pre-teen has heard at least one thing on every subject imaginable and is now smarter than mom and dad.

For those of you that have teenagers, this understanding will make sense to you now. It isn't that they aren't listening. It is that they have a critical faculty that rejects any idea that comes into play from the parent that is not in harmony with what they themselves have built on that perception. I see this in my own children as well, and it is a simple demonstration of how our minds work.

Tell a person who has depression that they are a worthy valuable person, and you'll see that critical faculty clamp down. Tell a person who has only known poverty that abundance is their birthright and wealth is more of a mindset then a number in a bank account and they will likely scoff at the idea.

Tell a person who has anxiety to trust the process of life and that life is there to support them and you'll see the same thing. A critical faculty protecting what's already there and not allowing anything new to enter that doesn't match what was there first. Again, what was there first was solidified between conception and the age of 5.

Now contrast that with this statement my mentor once said: If you want to make an alcoholic smile, tell him what a no-good low life piece of shit he is. I am not advising you to do this, but you get the idea.

They often will instantly, unconsciously, and unintentionally smile at that message because it matches a deep-down perception, they have of themselves: their self-image. Because it matches or resonates with something already planted in there, the critical faculty swings wide open allowing the message to pass right in. With that, a feeling of security added to that perception, even if it is unhealthy and not ideal, but enough to make them smile.

Plato's Allegory of the Cave shows a clear example of the critical faculty at work when the escaped prisoner was attempting to share his experience outside of the cave and the shadows that they have grown to understand as truth, was merely an illusion, yet the prisoners referred to him as imbecilic and a lunatic.

How many times have you seen this work in your life? Ever try to explain something to someone, even if that new idea could save their life or remove great misery from them and you can automatically feel their mind slam shut?

It is the critical faculty at work.

Sometimes people do not agree to the concept that everything goes back to the earliest years of childhood. Others may find it fascinating that the most powerful memories that essentially govern everything about us were formed so early, yet this is not even controversial.

In an interview involving Dr. Gabor Mate', he was asked, "Does everything go back to childhood? Can people experience a trauma at ages 16, 21, 29, or 33 that will impact them so severely as an adult?" He answers, "It is all about childhood." And to verify it, he cites a study on Post Traumatic Stress Disorder where it describes how out of one hundred soldiers who go into battle, roughly twenty will come out of the situation with PTSD while roughly eighty do not.

What is the reason for this? Simple. Of the twenty soldiers that show signs of PTSD, they were *also traumatized in childhood*. It was the adult experience that was responsible for triggering the previous recorded trauma from their childhood.

In other words, it was a re-triggering of the holographic wounding that was already there, and the experience simply reinforced and compounded the encoded data that was already there.

The same occurrence is also commonly found with concentration camp survivors. The people who experienced early childhood conditions which made them feel safe and supported, show much better chance of coming out of them without significant trauma symptoms. (16)

It all goes back to childhood because that is when our brain is developing, our personalities are forming, our foundational beliefs about us as well as everything, both positive and negative in the world, and how we feel about life are all viewed through this mindset.

From then on, we keep reacting to any of life's experiences through this mindset that behaves like a filter called a critical faculty. It all happens in early template of childhood and later as an adult, the performance of how we deal with any adversity that comes up is very much conditioned by how we were first raised and the conditions that we were in.

This law of compounding is important to understand because of the following reason: if a person is miserable and they *choose* not to do anything about it, in 5 years' time they will be even more miserable. If we do a brief review of my childhood chapter, it is easy to understand why all the compounding events from my earliest childhood, to moving in with my Aunt and Uncle, to the events in school, all led to my miserable state and self-destructive behavior by the time I was twenty years old.

Although taking steps towards a new direction in life is frightening, and the deepest, most powerful, and primal part of our brain wants to avoid pain and move toward pleasure (which is why most people do not change).

What is *more frightening* is staying where you are comfortable and not changing. The problem with this is when we are in the comfort zone, we may feel good staying precisely where we are at, *even if it is miserable*.

Remember how the law of compounding works, similar to gravity and over time, without changing, whatever you are feeling that drove you to read this book, will only build with time unless you choose to do something about it.

CHAPTER 6

The Development of Chronic Illness through Self-Mutilation Programs in the Subconscious Mind

"Trauma is personal. It does not disappear if it is not validated. When it is ignored or invalidated the silent screams continue internally heard only by the one held captive. When someone enters the pain and hears the screams healing can begin." – Danielle Bernock

Now that we've established the mind model and observed how perceptions are formed and protected by the critical faculty, let's look deeper at the mechanisms of what causes most people to develop chronic illness overtime.

The uncomfortable truth about the formation of chronic illness through childhood trauma.

Let me share with you a case of a patient who contacted me through referral and when I reviewed the client history form, under the "reason for seeking Psychosomatic care", she wrote "chronic Illness."

This 43-year-old female, Sarah (not her real name) reached out to us after she had undertaken a variety of natural remedies and had seen several Naturopathic and Functional Medicine doctors. There were improvements in her symptoms, less flare ups of joint pain, yet they still occurred when she is stressed or triggered, and her digestive upsets and fatigue were still severe.

When I regressed her to cause by asking her subconscious mind to take us to the key event that has everything to do with this manifestation of chronic illness, I said, "There's a feeling you have, a feeling inside of yourself; a feeling that you don't like. A feeling like you don't deserve to live in harmony, like you deserve to be punished. You've tried running, hiding, and avoiding this feeling and today is the day you face it and become free from it. As you think about this feeling, becoming absorbed into it, there's a place in your body where you notice it most. First impression: Where do you feel that feeling coming from?"

She points to her stomach.

I continue. "As you focus on this feeling in your stomach, I want your subconscious mind to take you all the way back to the very first scene the very first circumstance the very key event that has everything to do with this feeling that you don't like."

Now in this case often times a person does not always regress us right back to the key event initially. It may take us to various events between the age range of 12 to 21 to an experience that was similar to the seed planting but not the very core initial imprint, which is what we must find to be successful long term. Anything other than finding the original seed planting of the problem is still treating at the surface level and the symptoms are likely to regrow back.

So, I usually must do a little detective work to determine if we are there or not.

As she described the characteristics of the holographic memory imprint, we regressed right back into the scene until she arrived at the moment, I asked her subconscious to take us to.

Me: First impression, in this moment your mind has taken you to, are you inside or are you outside?

Sarah: Inside.

Me: Are you alone or with people?

Sarah: There's two people. It is my parents.

Me: Is it daytime or nighttime?

Sarah: It's dark so maybe nighttime.

Me: In this moment your mind has taken you to, I want you to become aware of your hands. Observe your hands and notice the size of your hands. Look at the front and look at the back of your hands and as you observe them you, will get an idea of your age in this moment. How old are you in this moment?

Sarah: (In a surprised way) They are tiny! Very tiny hands! I'm a newborn!

Me: In this moment your mind is taken you to when you're a newborn, inside and you're with your parents and it's dark, give me a report and share with me what you're sensing in this moment.

Sarah: I'm in my crib and I can see my parents standing outside of my crib and I hear them talking. (suddenly my patient's face changes as she begins to sob uncontrollably with tears coming from her eyes)

Me: What are you becoming aware of in this moment?

Sarah: They don't want me!

Me: What is being said? What gives you this impression?

Sarah: She's arguing very loudly with my father. She just said that she didn't want to get pregnant and they're fighting. (crying becomes much more intense) They're both yelling, and she says, "This is a mistake" (crying continues to get intense but much more pain filled now as my patient cries out loud" I'm a mistake!! I'm a mistake!"

Ladies and gentlemen, this is what the most overlooked and foundational underlying issue in most chronic illnesses looks like.

Using regression to cause I have seen this type of scenario shown to me more times than I care to count. This scenario is what also originates a self-mutilation program that operates within the goal achieving subconscious mind and it does so with ruthless efficiency-- even for decades.

Therefore, the general cause for a majority of chronic diseases illnesses and various disorders of all kinds is simply the <u>execution of a goal achieving subconscious mind calling for self-mutilation or punishment.</u> As bold as this claim may seem, stay with me; this will all make more sense very soon.

This is precisely why all the good or all the damage to a child's template and self-image is solidified between the ages of conception and the age of five. These kinds of talks, perhaps arguments, between parents about the child begin as early as the scene we just witnessed and often times, are ongoing to a degree. It's pretty much written in stone that a child listening to all this is going to have heard about every imaginable comment describing who they are, what they deserve, what life has for them and their place in life by around the age of four.

Whatever the total sum of mom or dad's overall energy and intentions towards the child throughout these early years is of utmost importance. This book will illustrate more details on how thoughts are capable of influencing objects beyond our physical body, including infants and children.

If it is mostly that of fear the child's presence is too much of a burden to handle, that child's self-worth mutates quickly, and the perception begins to form that mom and dad would be better off if the child was never conceived. The result is a **self-mutilation program**, a subconscious perception originated from early childhood experiences responsible for a number of chronic illnesses (like Sarah's) which include chronic pain, autoimmune conditions and cancer.

Unfortunately, in our society, this kind of message gets tossed around carelessly, freely and frequently throughout the early years. What perception is there by 4 to 5 years old will have been compounded so many times that the child's critical faculty is now completely sufficient to protect those perceptions of self. All of this gets discovered and confirmed over and over in our clinical practice.

Over the years as a psychosomatic doctor, I can tell you that I have witnessed chronically ill patients, including ones with cancer, regress to moments in the womb and from this, are able hear the details of conversations between the mother and father over keeping the child or having an abortion. After everything else has failed to resolve their issues, they contact me, often as a last resort, and my efforts are focused on helping people go to past memories and experiences that they didn't know they had to go to get free from the things that are running their lives.

The reason I decided to describe this particular type of clinical case study with you is to emphasize a very powerful point: *thought is the seed of condition*. Seeds that take root early in childhood life and develop into symptoms overtime will regrow not only if treated at the surface level but even if treated anywhere else in the realm of secondary sensitizing events.

I have, interviewed, met and worked with many aspiring doctors of all kinds including Functional Medicine, Naturopath and Integrative Specialist who are convinced that our current medical model is a disease management model, therefore is flawed in its approach and a more natural approach is the appropriate way.

Many people who are suffering and looking for a way to heal themselves feel the same way regarding allopathic medicine and these people seeking out a natural course of care begin an endeavor, chasing remedy after remedy after supplement after herb and various other therapies and treatments looking for that answer.

The problem with this approach is that they are looking for an answer that is *outside* of themselves and they are never going to find it.

Let me be clear. I do recognize the importance of good nutrition, intelligent use of whole food supplements (not synthetic, lab manufactured vitamins) and usage of certain remedies when appropriate. What I am pointing out that the answer to heal must come from within. Healing from any chronic illness begins from the inside.

As Dr Bruce Lipton has said, "Your thoughts are more powerful than any medicine that exists on this planet" which means that healing starts within the mind.

If a person is not healing, they are *not a vibrational match* with healing to some degree. This means that some part of their internal world and their external world is not aligned properly. By internal world, I am referring to the subconscious mind.

The reason long term healing doesn't occur is because of misalignments. The external world and the internal world do not line up because there are parts of their internal world that aren't lined up. Remember the cases of the diabetics I shared earlier? How through the process of gathering information on nutrition and lifestyle changes we could change their outer world and it provided short term improvements? Why only short term? Because their internal world remained unchanged.

Please don't confuse the internal world, which is a subconscious program running, for a person consciously, actively, and enthusiastically wanting to improve their life. What's desired on the outside world will doubtfully change what has been programmed into the subconscious mind during the earliest moments of life.

Recall what you learned from Allegory of the Cave? Understand that any internal perceptions, no matter how potentially dangerous, set on self-destruction or unhealthy they are, are protected by the critical faculty.

Their internal world remained unchanged despite the methods we used which included Acupuncture, Contact Reflex Analysis, Muscle testing, Body Code, Emotional Code, various breathing exercises, meditation, Bio Energetic Synchronization Technique Level III, Emotional Clearing, Homeopathy and Quantum Integration methods. Despite my best efforts, using these techniques, I was still treating at the surface level, even if I was working within the person's subconscious mind. I was not treating the *seed* of when the thought was first planted. I was only treating at the stem, branches, and leaves, so to speak. That is why the improvements we witnessed, over time on multiple occasions, only lasted short term. The deeper calling for these symptoms remained.

To be clear, if you don't go back to the very first seed planting of when the problem first started in the mind, all other therapies can go on indefinitely. It is when you go back to the **Initial Sensitizing Event**, which is the very first scene, situation or event when the developing baby was in the womb, a newborn or a young infant and was *first was exposed to the problem* — and change it there — then like a domino falling over; each and every branch within the subconscious mind that originated from that initial event, falls away.

What I witnessed clinically with my diabetic patients was not an anomaly either. During this time, I also interviewed dozens of colleagues who were also clinical directors of their own practice, using Functional Medicine and many of them shared that they also noticed short term improvements in most of their patients, some more than others.

A few of these doctors recognized that there "was something missing", to quote a female New York Functional Medicine doctor I interviewed. This was despite the fact that we were doing the most sophisticated lab work on the planet, including a 16-page DNA analysis from a stool sample that gave the most accurate readout of the gut microbiome available.

I interviewed the most seasoned Naturopathic Doctor in the proximal region of Kansas City regarding adrenal fatigue in women of childbearing age and he simply said, "Oh yes, you'll see a lot of them" without any other explanation to *why* other than to give them adrenal supporting nutraceuticals.

Further investigations through interviews as well as asking several mentors (who had taught me the previous techniques), all led to similar conclusions. On one of these occasions, I was having lunch with a mentor who taught me how to be proficient with muscle testing. This included Dr Versendaal's method known as Contact Reflex Analysis, and during our meeting, I asked him, "Do you ever notice that patients seem to have symptoms disappear when we find a problem and treat it to only have them return shortly after with another problem?"

This pattern was one that troubled me, and my mentor, a Diplomat in B.E.S.T., a lead instructor to several doctors on clinical applications as well as a very seasoned and brilliant Chiropractor from Kansas, nodded his head and indicated that he was also very familiar with this pattern. At nearly 70 years old, he had decades of experience ahead of me. He calmy responded with, "Yes. That happens. It is good job security."

His answer shook me to my core as I instinctively knew deep down that, although what we were doing was much safer than the allopathic approach (the number 3 cause of death in people today) (17), we were still not really helping our patients to the degree that I felt was necessary for *complete* healing to take place.

Despite being the "natural" doctors, applying the best nutritional supplements and using the absolute most cutting-edge approaches and techniques, we were in fact still treating symptoms — not the root cause.

Were these isolated incidents? Far from it. Dr Drouin M.D. from Quantum University once said, "98% of doctors who use natural approaches have taken an allopathic approach into their practice." An uneasy feeling grew in my stomach as I realized this resonated with truth and my practice reflected this.

If this wasn't enough, I also noticed the same thing in myself.

As I mentioned in earlier chapters, my childhood traumas being the origination from my PTSD, and only to be proliferated from my time in the Marine Corps, I too noticed that despite my own PTSD protocols, including thyroid, hypothalamus, pituitary, and adrenal overhaul-- as well as countless sessions of emotional clearing--my own PTSD remained.

The improvements were very short lived although I did have a moment of calm after an acupuncture session or a B.E.S.T. adjustment, yet there was still something under the surface that remained.

I was still easily triggered and the anger and unconscious pain I had carried my entire life would rise back to the surface after a period of time. I would do a session on clearing anger yet found myself feeling emotions of anger after very minor incidents. I was working on my subconscious mind, yet what I was unaware of that it was *surface level work* in the part of my mind.

After my treatments I received, including Hypnosis, NLP, Emotional Freedom Technique, Body Code/ Emotional Code, I noticed my own symptoms of PTSD, anxiety and panic attacks returning shortly after. There were some improvements, but symptoms of flashbacks, nervousness, occasional bursts of anger and anxiety still remained.

Being unsatisfied with what I had concluded in my work as "treating symptoms" and surface level work and not addressing the root cause, I began to investigate further. This led to me shifting from a purely Functional Medicine and energy work approach and transitioning into Psychosomatic Medicine because it was becoming obvious to me it was all about the patient's internal self that was what we were missing.

A lot of times what we think is the cause and is the source of our symptoms, isn't.

The subconscious mind is not a linear type of mind such as the conscious mind. The conscious mind thinks like a bottle rocket type of trajectory where the subconscious mind processes information more akin to a cluster of grapes growing on a fence.

The reason the clinical nutrition, herbs, supplements and all the energy healing discipline that I mentioned, tended to not achieve the long term change I was going for in my practice was, *it only targeted 2/3 of the human being*. My approach (as well as my colleagues' approaches) targeted the physical body with nutritional protocols and directly on the energy body and for the most part, left the mental body untouched.

Ladies and gentlemen, the mental body is *the causative* body.

Let's examine this idea a little closer. Remember what the characteristics of the subconscious mind are? The most powerful goal achieving agency known to man. This combined with the inability to judge a single decision.

Well, although I was working with the subconscious mind, I was still working on surface level and additionally my methods were insufficient. I was not aware that the perceptions I was attempting to shift, were of a holographic nature and I was unintentionally leaving fragments behind.

Each fragment contained the entire memory, or perception so anytime a person would trigger a single fragment, the memory and the calling would revive itself and the symptoms would reappear.

There is a significant body of evidence that points out most chronic illness originate from childhood trauma including autoimmune diseases, cancer, and degenerative nervous system disorders and so on because of the unshakable and unalterable *connection between the mind and body*. (18)

This will make much more sense as it is explained later in this chapter but first, we should briefly ease into observing how our current view of the nature of us and our world originated. The reason for this is that there is currently a *conflict* within the heart of science between two worlds.

So, we should recognize that although we may hear the common phrase, "The science is settled" we should at least recognize that this "science" view has spread throughout the entire world, is the basis of the education systems, National Health Service, Medical Research Council, and virtually all establishments of government operate under what we will refer to as a *mechanistic*, or material model.

In this original belief system, the mechanistic view, the idea is that *mind and matter are completely separate entities*.

Making the connection between the perceivable and recognizable, physical world and the inner mental world of thought has been a difficult task for both scientists, spiritual teachers, wise men and philosophers for quite some time and this debate has been ongoing since at least the time of the Greek philosopher Plato.

He was amongst the first to argue that the human mind was an entity unto itself existing separately from the physical body.

Within the Western world mechanistic view, science has established this belief over centuries time until the very foundation became the accepted and established perspective: the mind is nothing more than the sum of the physical brain's electrical and biochemical activity.

Is it any wonder why people today still would find it difficult to contemplate the notion that their thoughts can somehow shape their life and their endeavors?

To achieve a paradigm shift of this old idea, a thorough understanding of how physical matter exists and originates is necessary.
To do this, not only do we need to have an open mind, but we also need to remember the *important function of the critical faculty* and how it will guard our held perceptions, even if those perceptions are inaccurate.

Having an open mind is also a good litmus test for how educated a person is. After all, the eyes are useless when the mind is blind, as my mentor used to say. I think you know that if we're going to improve any area of our life, we must have a very open mind. An open mind is best summarized by being prepared to throw away some of our most cherished beliefs when a better idea comes along.

Many of us have a false concept programmed into our mind with respect to education. I think we have been raised to believe that education is going to school for several years and after that, to be able to correctly answer a series of questions to determine what you have "learned."

Now, many people go to school for a decade and are able to correctly answer the questions but then when it comes to getting out into the marketplace and really accomplishing their dreams, their goals and successes, perhaps financial security, many times they just don't know how to make it happen. That is because they *gathered information* from the schooling, but not necessarily received an education.

Napoleon Hill in his phenomenal book *Think and Grow Rich* points out that missing link in all systems of education known to civilization today may be found in the failure of educational institutions to teach students how to organize and use knowledge after they acquire it.

We should understand the real meaning of the word educate. Contrary to what we may have been taught, education is not going to a brick-and-mortar edifice for several years. This is more accurately described as gathering information, not necessarily developing an education.

Note: I'm not against education, but it is far more important to understand how to develop the mind, as we have come to understand it from previous chapter. For this very reason my wife and I created a board accredited university, **Psychosomatic University**, where our students develop an understanding of the mind and at the same time, heal from their own traumas. (19)

The word "educate" comes from the Latin word *edu* or *educo* meaning "to induce to draw out or to develop from within something that is hidden or latent." (20)

In my career, I have known many colleagues who graduated from chiropractic college with me but are not living any better lives then they did before earning a degree. (In fact, one could argue that some are living *worse* from accumulated school debt) An educated person is not necessarily one who has the abundance of general or specialized knowledge. An educated person is one who has so developed the faculties of their mind that they may acquire anything they want or its equivalent without violating the rights of others. An educated person is the one that knows how to go and get what they want out of life, with a degree or not.

Sidney Herbert Wood, a British assistance secretary in the Ministry of Education, formulated a few questions to determine the presence of an educated person. One of these brilliant questions is "Can you entertain a new idea?" This question exposes the presence of the critical faculty at work because you'll find that the majority of people seem to pause and back up hesitatingly, dragging all of their old experience with them when they're confronted with a new idea.

Deep down an uncomfortable feeling stirs as the idea is closed off by the protective barrier of the subconscious mind. They ask themselves, "Does this new idea fit?" If it doesn't fit, they say *it's wrong* within a fraction of a second and this all happens below the surface of their conscious awareness.

I am going to invite you to have an open mind as we observe this conflict that is still present in our society. A conflict of mind and matter being separate altogether; a concept that needs to be met head on.

In modern times, there is a widespread delusion that scientific authorities, governments, and the health care system still hold onto. It is more accurately described as a belief system then it is a true scientific inquiry.

This system is based on unwavering, restricted beliefs that originated from the seventeen hundreds and unfortunately, has not changed much. For example, if you have a grandmother that was formerly trained as a nurse and you currently have a daughter that is also studying to be a nurse, the course work involving biology sciences that they are studying, likely has not changed at all. They are most likely studying from the same textbooks, although they may be newer condition, or "updated" versions, the information likely has not changed.

I witnessed this firsthand in my own educational journey. During my studies at Chiropractic college, our biochemistry professor put enormous effort on us learning the aspects of cellular respiration, and particularly, the Kreb-cycle, a complex series of reactions of on how our body makes energy from food. It was not long after I graduated that I heard Dr Bruce Lipton, a PhD and brilliant cellular biologist discussing that the Kreb cycle we learned was completely obsolete and the information we essentially learned was from an outdated model.

Unfortunately, this held belief system is the current worldview and has even come so far as to inhibit and compress the free inquiry which is the very core of the scientific endeavor. A brief view of the tremendous widespread censorship that has occurred over the last several years is a blatantly obvious example of this. We are suddenly witnessing "fact checkers" show up in various aspects of social media, a clear sign of restriction of scientific inquiry.

Let's peer closer into this how this original, dogmatic belief system came into acceptance.

Born on March 31st, 1596 was the French philosopher, scientist and mathematician Rene Descartes, who was widely considered a key figure in the origination of modern philosophy, science, mathematics with his ability to merge separate fields of algebra and geometry into analytic geometry (21).

His famous statement "cogito, ergo sum" or "I think therefore I am" was one that still resides in classrooms today, as does his tremendous contribution to mathematics and other similar fields.

Although his findings contributed greatly to the developments in the fields of mathematics, this current held dogmatic belief, was based on one of his theories: A theory that the universe was a mechanistic, machine-like system and that it operated under this mechanical type of behavior.

Centuries later, this has become the default worldview of most educational systems which simply implies that the universe is like a machine. This includes animals and plants as well as us. According to Richard Dawkins, we are little more than "lumbering robots." This view also implies that our brains are little more than genetically programmed computers.

By the age of 23, Descartes was highly motivated and driven to develop a scientific method of reasoning which would apply to any field of information and from it, would offer readily available demonstrations of how the universe worked. Only when the results within every scientific inquiry were predictable and certain as the ones achieved in mathematics did Descartes feel that his theory would hold true. When it came to human nature, he found that the physical and mental arenas were completely separate from one another.

Descartes noted that thought itself, was not of the scientific inquiry, but it belonged exquisitely to the human soul.

It seemed that human mind held an excessive number of shifting quantities and inconsistencies that did not confine to any laws or predictable outcomes regarding the mechanistic model. The confusion in him when attempting to blend the mechanical, predictable outer world with the inconsistencies and unpredictable nature of the human mind, Descartes made the bold claim that the human mind was outside of the boundaries that operated within the mechanistic and material physical laws.

This led to the beginning of the dogmatic, held belief system that still remains today. It is that mind and matter were not the same nor were they to even be comparable to each other. Matter was the jurisdiction of science and therefore the mind is under the jurisdiction of religion.

Descartes works commenced this belief, that still plagues us today, that confine the mind as an entirely different entity than matter, including our physical body. He rejected the splitting of corporal substance into matter and form taking it as far as documenting his works in *The Passion of the Soul* "as if no one had written on these matters before."

This view stood as the recognized and accepted foundation for how our universe operates for hundreds of years and there were other figures who added solidity to this view.

Amongst those figures and originator of what has been commonly referred to as Newtonian physics comes Sir Isaac Newton, born in December 1642. The English mathematician, scientist, physicist, and alchemist was considered a key figure in the Scientific Revolution. His works including the published book *Mathematical Principles of Natural Philosophy*, solidified influential beliefs in the classical mechanic theory and this greatly contributed to the belief that the universe operated more along the lines of a mechanical and predictable machine-like behavior.

Considered one of the most influential scientists in history, his model of Newtonian Physics was flawed in one, perhaps devastating way: *that all known matter in our material world was made from solid atoms.* In this way, energy was defined simply as capacity to do work. It was limited to being a force to move objects, but that was it.

This viewpoint not only limits our understanding of what energy is, but it greatly downplays the importance and the implications for which it possesses.

Note: As a traditional trained Chiropractor, we were taught this view as energy only being a force, in which we used to manipulate spinal segments, a term used by chiropractors as an adjustment. Anything else beyond energy's ability to be used as a means for healing was considered *pseudoscience* by the academic authorities, was greatly discouraged and not to be discussed in any formal setting.

This demonstrates the very conflict I previously pointed out between a belief system, held onto and acts on inhibiting and constricting the very lifeblood of what is true scientific endeavor and a method of investigation based on reason, evidence, formulated hypothesis and collective investigation.

All my post educational work I mentioned previously involving energy healing was completely detached from the academic setting, a clear sign that the dogmatic beliefs are still very much a part of our education, including our health care system.

It is important to point this out because, as you will soon read, energy is the very foundation for everything and is responsive to mind and thought energy. Remember *the mental body is the causative body* in cases of virtually all chronic illness.

The relevance of this is vitally important to understand because the result of this established belief system put forth by Descartes and Newton that the nature of our universe and everything in it functions by a mechanical like operation, this implies that we as people *have little to no influence on changing our results*. It means that all our reality, including our health, happiness and our wealth—is all predetermined and operates in a machine-like manner with us having no ability to influence it or change it.

Have you ever thought to yourself or known someone that you care about deeply that seems to think, "Why bother trying?" or "What is the use?" This kind of mindset comes from the very foundation of deeply held beliefs that our thoughts, our beliefs and/or our actions do not seem to matter and will not create any notable change.

Think about this for a moment. Have you ever blamed anyone for anything in the last year? We get mad perhaps at the president or the economy or the oil prices. We blame other people for our lack of reaching success. We blame our parents. We blame our boss. We blame our co-workers.

Many people carry this burden within themselves, and as the time goes by, they eventually identify themselves as victims in a cruel game of life.

This is a very subtle and nasty insinuation. How? Because it entices us to keep doing things that we do in which we really don't like doing, such as living in misery, poverty or being chronically sick. Likewise, it prevents us from doing the things that we would really like to do, such as building the business we dream of, writing the book we imagine doing, finding the right and healthy relationship we desire or going on the dream vacation that seems beyond our limits.

If we believe this materialistic view and with that, we feel like we have no power and are limited by only what our current results reflect, this means that we are currently all we are ever going to be.

In other words, we are settling for what we are today. If you are looking at the results in your life or your health and you are unsatisfied with them, this should be a disturbing thought.

If we have the internal drive to do more and be more, along with relentless determination, motivation and we gain the proper education, we're going to be led into some very wise decisions that will inspire us into some intelligent action and we will live a very fulfilled life.

Speaking of education, let us revisit these notions once more. The mechanistic view implies that all physical matter is just that; physical matter that is unconscious and solid.

The whole universe is composed from unconscious matter with no consciousness in stars, galaxies, animals, plants, water and there ought not to be any in us either if this theory is true. So, a lot of the philosophy in this mechanistic model over the last several hundreds of years has been trying to prove that we're not conscious at all (22).

With matter being unconscious then the laws of nature are fixed, unalterable and constant. This means that the laws now in place are the same as the moment the big bang occurred.

This fit the model of a mechanistic and machine-like universe. However, what does the evidence say? Does this understanding hold up to scientific inquiry?

Despite this view being the dominate, default view that reigns over our educational systems today, there is more to the story then we are being told. A new story is emerging.

It seems like there is a field of consciousness, or awareness, that extends through all of space. Our universe, and everything in it, is a *thinking* universe.

To see some examples of this, first let's take a closer look at stars. Could they just be burning balls of gas without consciousness? According to the *Journal of Consciousness Exploration and Research,* Stars may actually be thinking entities that deliberately control their own paths [23].

Next, let's look at plants. In 1966, Cleve Baxter was America's foremost lie detector expert and examiner. He operated a school that taught law enforcement, FBI agents and security agents from around the world the art of lie detection.

Acting on an intuitive impulse after he had been up all night in his school for polygraph examiners, he decided to attach the electrodes of one of his lie detectors to the leaf of a dracaena, a tropical plant related to the palm tree.

He was attempting to see if he could get a reaction from the plant physiology which would be recorded on his polygraph machine. In his own words, "The most effective way to trigger in a human being a reaction strong enough to make the galvanometer jump is to threaten his or her well-being." Baxter's curiosity drove him to attempt this on a plant.

First, he dunked the leaf of addressing area in a cup of hot coffee perennially in his hand as he observed the machines readout. There was no reaction displayed on the galvanometer readout.

Baxter analyze the problem several minutes and then conceived a worse and more threatening idea. He decided he would burn the actual leaf of where the electrodes were attached.

Astonishingly, the instant he had the picture of the flame in his mind and before he could even reach for a match there was a dramatic change in the tracing pattern on the graph in the form of a significant prolonged upward sweep (24).

For animals, we need only to review the previous chapter discussing the mind model and the experiments done with Renee Pe'och and the baby chickens.

Let's visit the fascinating nature of water. In Germany, the Stuttgart Aerospace Institute has discovered a fascinating way of photographing information stored within water. Using a large apparatus containing water they successfully demonstrated that by dipping a flower into the water and then removing it, that the water stored information from the flower within every single droplet.

This shows us another example of our existence within a holographic reality, being formatted in a way that every part of a hologram is a smaller version of the whole. The base form of this reality, as we will soon learn, is not solid pieces of atomic building blocks, like the Newtonian Physics model represented.

It is composed of waveform information and patterns of different vibrations or frequencies.

Next, the Institute invited people from the local community to the lecture hall and gave them all individual dishes with their names written on it. The researchers then placed four droplets from the same source of water within each dish, collected all the dishes and proceeded to examine them more closely. They discovered that each individual person, who had their own dish containing four droplets of water from the same source produced different images from the same water. (25)

Moreover, the works of Dr Luc Montagnier, the joint recipient of the 2008 Nobel Prize in Physiology for the discovery of HIV, opened the doors further on the concept of water memory by discovering that the blood plasma from patients infected with HIV, he detects unforeseen, unique electromagnetic signals, something that was never witnessed until then.

In fact, this kind of phenomenon wasn't even considered by classical biology. In his own words, Dr Montagnier explained, "I've always been searching for the extraordinary. I find it hard to work on an established theory. I'd rather innovate."

Another more famous example is by the New York Times Best Seller Dr Masaru Emoto, and his book *The Hidden Messages in Water*.

212

His experiments show that thought energy from human consciousness directed at water can change the molecular structure. His students would imagine the idea of negative thoughts or energy in various ways of insulting gestures and direct it at specific water containers.

Then, they would imagine positive, encouraging ideas and direct each positive emotion towards other containers of water.

Next, they would freeze it to 20° below 0 and place it under a microscope. As they examined the water with negative thought energy directed at it, they found irregular blobby, black formations.

When the students sent positive emotions, such as love, gratitude or thank you, they examined beautiful, proportional crystals that look like snowflakes. One kind of energy which is negative critical energy creates one type of structure in water, while positive and uplifting energy creates an entirely different type of structure.

These theories provide additional evidence that water is capable of responding to human presence, thoughts and emotions. This would not be possible if thought was only confined within the brain.

In the case of human beings, the materialistic, mechanical model indicates that we are nothing more than are flesh robots; solid objects at the atomic level.

Most of us only have to think back to the days in our 5th grade scientific classroom where we used little colored wooden circles connected by dal rods mimicking the structure of atoms. It was during these moments using wooden models that we were taught atoms were solid objects and they were the building blocks of all matter. This of course includes us as our body is composed of 50 to 70 trillion cells, and each cell is composed of 100 trillion atoms. It is the foundation of this mechanistic mechanical view, and it became the standard of how we were (and still are) taught of how the universe operates and functions.

Recall in a previous paragraph when I mentioned a new story is emerging that shows something else? This new story is not exactly "new" as it began in October of 1927, and it would change everything we understood of our physical universe.

It began in the Solvay Institute Building, located in Belgium and the matters discussed involve the nature of these fundamental particles which make up the world we see around us. It was here that Einstein amongst many others, entered a heated debate that would lead to the discovery of quantum entanglement.

Over the period of a week, a series of discussions took place closely examining the nature of matter and the new quantum theory.

This photograph shows a collection of some of the most brilliant people in the world, the pioneers of quantum mechanics and this was one of the greatest meetings of scientific minds in history. More than half were already or would soon become Nobel Prize winners. Their experiments were showing that deep inside the matter, tiny particles of atoms with orbiting electrons, were *not* solid little spheres as they once believed. Instead of solid matter, they seemed to be fuzzy and undefined.

This exploration ushered in new territory in exploring including the puzzling behavior of light and its seemingly unpredictable ability to shift from a wave, which is not solid, instantly into a solid particle. How it does this *is the very foundation of this chapter regarding self-mutilation programs* and their role in the development of chronic disease.

These scientists were the ones responsible for exploring deeper and deeper to find what they hope would have been the bedrock of the world that they live in. To their shock and surprise, they found things less and less solid. As they explored deeper into this world, there were no tiny little "bricks" that got smaller. In contrast, at some point the bricks gave way to this "cloudy mush" and what appeared like solidity and solidness, in fact became very confusing and originated a whole new way of thinking about nature.

Albert Einstein, born in Germany, March 1879 is widely regarded as one of the greatest and most influential scientists of all time. Not only was his theory of relatively a significant contribution but also his important contribution to quantum mechanics.

At this meeting, he shared his famous equation of E=Mc2, which means Energy equals mass times the speed of light squared. This equation proved that energy was not just a force to work, but it was so fundamentally related to this "cloudy mush" that makes up physical matter.

Energy and matter are simply the inverse of each other and not separated.

These findings completely contradicted the Newtonian Physics model; dismissed and proved that what was once held as the understood belief, was in fact, completely incorrect.

Obviously, the Newtonian Physics theory was faulty at the very core at which it stood on; that all known physical material was solid. In exploring within the subatomic world composed of electrons protons and neutrons, it became obvious that our so-called physical world is composed of two primary substances: *waves*, which are energy and solid physical *particles*.

Now, whether it is a wave, or a particle *is dependent on the mind of the observer*. Remember when I said the mental body is the causative body? Soon, we will go more into this. To understand how our universe, including our lives and our body, functions, we must first understand the behavior of the tiniest components within it, the atoms and the energy from which they are made up of.

When we begin the techniques later, it will be very important for you to first understand this: Everything physical in your life is composed of this "cloudy mush" that is not a solid matter at all. It is composed of fields of energy and vibrational patterns of information. To summarize this, Max Planck said it best. "The stuff of our world does not exist the way we think it exists."

It was not just Descartes and Newton who contributed to us viewing ourselves as victims in a world that seemed so separate from our truest self.

In the words of Lynne McTaggart, "Everything in the entire universe, including the atom models we learned about in 5th grade science class, derives its meaning from their relationships and these relationships are part of a larger interconnected make up of pure consciousness. Each of us is a part of something so much bigger than we realize.

Everything we believe about our world and our place within it takes its lead from the ideas that were formulated in the 17th century...."

"Our self-image grew… bleaker with the work of Charles Darwin. His theory of evolution… is a life that is random, predatory, purposeless, and solitary… you are no more than an evolutionary accident… as The Pioneers of quantum physics peered into the very heart of the matter, they were astounded by what they saw. The tiniest bits of matter… these subatomic particles had no meaning in isolation, but only in a relationship with everything else… you could understand the universe as a dynamic web of interconnection."
(26)

Max Karl Planck, a German theoretical physicist born in 1858, is considered the "father" of quantum theory. His works contributed greatly to theoretical physics, but his fame was as the originator of quantum theory which completely revolutionized our understanding of the functioning in atomic and subatomic processes.

His quote of, "As a man who is devoted his whole life to the most clear-headed science to the study of matter, I can tell you as a result of my research about the atoms this much. *There is no matter as such!*"

This means that the way that we perceive our world, and our very existence does not function the way we may believe it exists. He goes on to say that what we perceive as matter in our physical world, "originates and exists by a force." This force is an intelligent, thinking, and responsive field of energy that holds everything together.

Now, Earlier I said that the wave or particle is dependent on the mind of the observer. Initially, there was confusion when the scientist peered into this cloudy mush because it was unpredictable in how they appeared and how it behaved.

When the scientists began to observe and calculate the subatomic enclosure, they noticed that the laws of physics did not apply to this smaller world. It is easy to understand and even buy into the material and mechanical theory because of the behavior of larger objects, like a tennis ball bouncing, a tire rolling on a vehicle and a rock being thrown and breaking a glass window or splashing in water. These are all easy to duplicate, are reliable and anticipated.

However subatomic components, such as electrons, behaved quite differently. The interactions within this mushy cloud, they appeared and disappeared, losing, and gaining mass at will and in ways that are completely outside of how the much larger world appears.

It appeared as though the particles, which are matter, only appeared very temporary to disappear completely. What the physicist soon realized was that the act of observing it, is what effects the difference between if it shows up as energy or if it shows up as matter. Further experiments concluded that electrons exist simultaneously by appearing and disappearing all within an infinite number of possibilities or chances in this invisible field of energy.

Now, here is where it really becomes fascinating.

It only converts to a physical matter, or particle, when a witness, or observer, focuses their attention within any location with the expectancy, or belief that something is there. This means a particle will only manifest when we are looking in expectation for it.

Quantum Physicist Amit Goswami called this the "collapsing of the particle", and he also pointed out it has tremendous implications. As it is also coined, **the observer effect**, it means that when we are looking for an electron, (or any possibility) there is a specific location within the field of energy where the subatomic world arranges itself to form that electron into a physical substance.

A very important point to understand here: it means that *the mind and matter are completely one* in the same. They are not separate from each other. As you will see in the following chapters, it is this mind that produces objective changes in the physical world and by now, I assume you understand that reason the day-old chicken was able to influence a mechanical robot.

You should also understand the reason the mind is responsible for a majority of developing chronic illness. With this understanding, know that it is thought that creates our destiny. *If things go wrong in our life, it is an act of mind.*

How would your life completely transform if you realized that your thoughts, or participation of the observer effect, are causing all the things to happen in your life to you and just by shifting your focus onto something else, can directly impact the direction of your life?

This means that you can begin to observe a different circumstance in your life, dropping the mindset that your thoughts and actions do not matter, to grasping the fact that they absolutely create your reality!

Sounds great, right? No one can do it for you, as we are all creators of our own life. Yes, this book will help you drop a significant amount of subconscious weight and rechange the coding system in your mind, but unless you are willing to understand that we create our reality, this book (or any book, seminar, or technique) will be of little use.

It is critical that we learn the power of our mind and use it accordingly. This means we develop the mindset of being solution orientated rather than a complainer. We must give up *all* excuses and justifications for why we did not achieve our results or defending our positions that are not resulting in improvements in our life.

We must train ourselves to see only the positive in every circumstance we are dealt. We must give up all the blaming of others and take 100% responsibility for our life. We also need to understand this fundamental truth: *forgiveness is the real healer*. I am aware that this idea may bring up a variety of thoughts feelings and emotions. Perhaps this thought makes perfect sense to you now understanding how important thoughts actually are. Does it make sense intellectually? Maybe part of you is thinking it's absurd to even consider a ridiculous notion? Perhaps you may have had a flash of someone's face come across your mind just at the thought of forgiving.

I'm wide aware that a person can be anywhere on that spectrum when I say that forgiveness is the healer. To anyone having trouble with that statement let me explain. Please know that I feel that this is the most important thing to know if you are looking to heal a condition that implies something "is eating away at you." Forgiveness is the healer and at the exact opposite end of the spectrum is *judgment*, whether it's judgment of ourselves, some action we did (or did not do) or of someone else. Forgiveness heals while judgment creates illness, suffering and a slow painful death.

Some of the most powerful perception shifts I've ever witnessed clinically come through getting a person out of judgment and into forgiveness. When we regress to cause and find a situation in which somebody's wronged us, the objective is to diffuse any contempt and make sense out of the experience find peace, learn, heal and grow.

Forgiveness is the lubricant that frees the person to do exactly that. Something I want to point out is that *forgiveness has nothing to do with the condoning action*. Many people get confused at this. Perhaps someone has really done you wrong in the past. Oftentimes they assume that forgiving them, that you're condoning the action and that is not the case at all.

Remember it's your thoughts that create your reality. This is where it all starts.

Forgiveness has nothing to do with the condoning action. Forgiveness is acknowledging that a person doesn't act that way because of what is happening *to them*. A person acts that way because of what is happening *inside of them*. By forgiving a person *you set yourself free* from the implications of his or her act.

It is important to see how far this extends, as your mind interacts with every atom in your body and your life. Your reality is not the cause of your thoughts and your feelings, but your thoughts and your feelings are in fact what is creating your reality.

The field of energy that makes up all our cells in our body, responds to our mind and thoughts and forms into all physical matter. Within this field, often referred to as Zero Point Field, scientist as well as the Quantum Model tells us that *all possibilities exist.*

This means a version of you that is happy, healthy, and wealthy already exist as potentials ready to come into existence by observing them. Everything is there including the greatest suffering or the greatest joys and triumphs.

Belief is the code that translates the invisible energy (waves of possibilities) into Max Planck's Matrix into visible Matter. (particles of physical matter)

Now, let us look further into beliefs.

There are beliefs you know about and beliefs that you do not know about. This may be the most important concept to understand in this entire book. We will cover this more in depth in the upcoming chapters, however for now understand that it is the beliefs that we do *not* know about that are holding us back and preventing us from accessing this field of infinite possibilities. You see, your dominant beliefs are not the ones that you are thinking right now. They are not the ones you are aware of.

Your dominate beliefs are the thoughts, feelings, lessons and distinctions held at the subconscious level that are always running and it doesn't really matter what you do or understand consciously until you find a way to change that.

We must get those in harmony and get those vibrating on the same frequency all going in the same direction and then suddenly, tremendous shifts start to take place in your life.

The things that hold a person back from achieving anything in their life, including healing, to a large part are not their fault.

When you have an experience in the infancy of your life, it's recorded holographically throughout the entire nervous system and the causal body is where that memory information is stored and it's running on a perpetual loop similar to a little pocket dimension and it generates a surcharge of emotional energy because that fragment of your consciousness doesn't know that event is over.

Recall the trauma mechanism we discussed in chapter 4? If that pocket of consciousness is not properly addressed and resolved, the symptoms will always find a way to resurface because the cause is not addressed.

These statements had everything to do with what we were all missing and is the reason why our patients were not achieving the level of long-term healing that they were looking for.

Understand that there are always exceptions to this as what I am addressing here is the majority of what I witnessed through clinical practice, what I discovered through hours of investigating and what was apparent in my own life.

This understanding is what made me investigate regression work, because this is where the power to change our earliest experiences truly is! This is where you get the answers that go far beyond lab work and even the most sophisticated of muscle testing can provide. This is also the only approach that exists that gives us a pathway to locate the Initial Sensitizing Event (ISE).

Recall last chapter when we discussed the mind model and how we start out in this world knowing nothing of man; only the goodness of Divine bliss, light, and harmony, love, peace with zero burdens, and then comes along the moment of conception when we go from pure consciousness and pure light and then suddenly, we are compressed into a single cell.

At this moment we are still a single cell in the womb of mom yet all we still know is the perception of pure consciousness and Divine. As time passes, life events begin to happen so for most people that event comes in the form of an initial sensitizing event and that's when we go from only knowing the pureness of Divine to suddenly getting our first taste of humanity.

This is what I describe as a *pie in the face* because it goes from the moment when we're peaceful, harmonious, pure consciousness, only knowing the welcoming presence of Divine to suddenly out of nowhere, a pie smacks us in the face and we hear something along the line of Bruce Willis's voice saying, "Hey, welcome to the party pal!"

This is the moment that changes everything. It is the moment of separation from Divine because now we have a perception built which becomes the very foundation of our subconscious mind. It is also the most influential origination of who we are, how we view ourselves and what life has to offer us.

In my experience working with thousands of patients around the globe and completing nearly 5000 regressions-to-cause sessions with patients that have chronic illness, autoimmune conditions, chronic pain and a variety of physiological illnesses, the most common initial sensitizing event we find in our patients is when mom realizes that she is pregnant and she has a tremendous moment of regret, fear, and in some way, shape or form does not want the baby.

The subconscious mind builds a perception and over time and reinforced events, interprets this kind of circumstance as, "The most important people in the world, including mom and dad, don't want me around. They would be better off if I were dead."

Not a word of this accumulation of trauma is breathed in any of the medical, chiropractic or naturopathic school.

As a healer, my methods of being trained as a functional medicine doctor and chiropractor are no longer around adjusting segments of the spine, muscle testing and handing my patients a supplement or an herb, although there are exceptional moments when this is appropriate.

My approach today is to ask the only agency that knows the source of your problem, your subconscious mind, to take me to the very key event that has everything to do with the physical manifestation of your illness. I seek to find that underlying perception that is operating under your awareness and is tapping into a potential in the quantum field that you do not consciously consent for.

Much of my time is spent helping you go to places you didn't know you had to go, to locate this initial sensitizing event, and help you get free from the things that are running your life. The only source that knows where the origination from your chronic illness or chronic condition or chronic pain all began from the deepest pockets of your subconscious mind. Go anywhere else and you're wasting your time.

At the moment of conception is when you are the most absorbent and it is when you learn the most and it's these first initial memories that have tremendous influence and impact on you even decades later. It does not matter if you remember it consciously or not, your subconscious mind is the source of your long-term memory and remembers everything from the moment you were conceived until the present time. (27)

More often than not, when I regress my patients back to the first scene, situation or event that has everything to do with the reason they've contacted me, almost without exception, we spring back to a memory from in the womb up to around age 5 years old.

During a lecture, Dr Gabor Mate' says something that is so rich with truth. He said, "There's one major source of illness and I'm talking about any kind of illness whether that's so-called mental illness or physical illness and that's childhood trauma."

How does it work?

The subconscious mind is similar to a video camera that is always running but it runs in all five senses, so everything is recorded. When you come into this world you have no idea of what's right or wrong. You don't know good and bad. You have no sense of self until around age 4 or 5.

The ages between 0 to 5 are the most critical and powerful. This is exactly why whatever happens to mommy during this time, happens to you. If mom is stressed, you absorb and interpret every bit of this stress as if it yours. (27)

At this moment, you only know what feels *good* or feels *bad*. It's *familiar* or it's *unfamiliar*. I feel *safe* or I feel *threatened*.

For all practical purposes, you start out equivalent to a huge blank hard drive, with infinite storage capacity and no data. Whatever experience you have first, positive or negative, creates the ISE.

Instantly, this first perception (good or bad) becomes like a little magnet placed in your mind. The first experience is just recorded, not judged, not analyzed and it's not compared. It's just recorded and as you begin to accumulate more and more experiences they start to get grouped together by similarities.

These secondary experiences are called **Secondary Sensitizing Events** (SSEs)and as they begin to accumulate from life's' experiences, your subconscious mind begins to sort these accumulations of experiences by sameness. They don't have to be exactly alike. They could be 30% the same but they link and connect, in an unilinear pattern like a cluster of grapes forming a vast network. However, everything that comes after that primal and formal experience becomes the *standard by which everything else is measured by*.

On multiple occasions I have regressed a patient to moments after conception, when the ISE that they experienced was actually mom's encounter, which triggered a feeling or emotion, yet to a newly developing baby, they do not know the difference between what happens to mommy and what happens to them. So, it is essentially the same. That distinction between self and other (like mom) does not happen until later in life.

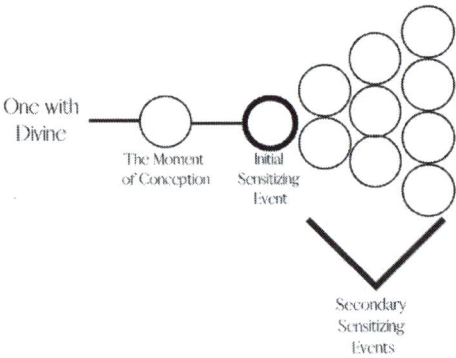

One with
Divine

The Moment
of Conception

Initial
Sensitizing
Event

Secondary
Sensitizing
Events

Remember the Law of compounding? Each one of these experiences that we have are like little magnetic links that we hang other experiences on and from that moment on as we begin to have more and more SSEs, the perception builds and builds in strength.

In the cases of most chronic illnesses, regressions take us back to a moment when the initial sensitizing event turns out to be some fear-based action by the parents that makes the developing baby in the womb, the infant, or the child feel as though mom and dad would be much happier or better off if the infant was never born.

I promise you this is one thing that remains amazingly consistent when looking at the self-image and the deep-down feelings that people with chronic diseases have about themselves when they feel like they don't deserve life, they don't deserve healing, they don't love themselves and the world would be better off if they were just gone.

Understanding this now gives you a better idea of why, if we correct things on the outside world, it has very little impact on the inside world because we are essentially playing chess with a subconscious mind that's programmed that the world would be better off if this person was just gone.

This lays down the blueprints a self-mutilation and it is very consistent amongst those with chronic illness when they have exhausted all methods of healing, tried every modality, used every protocol, has been seen by a dozen doctors and yet still remain chronically ill.

Take for example, I had a medical doctor, Charles (not his real name) who had heard me on a podcast and resonated with my message. He sought me out for chronic joint pain. I was explaining how the mind model works and I decided to ask him about his approach with his patients in helping them with their pain. I said, "Do you always use steroid injections?" to which he replied with," Yes." I asked, "Out of 100 or so steroid injections how often do you see the patient return in the near future requiring more injections?" He said, "All of them."

Incredible! I thought to myself as it had confirmed what I have witnessed in my own profession and amongst my own colleagues.

It was from this moment on we had a delightful conversation in which he went to explain that he had actually started in medicine looking for relief from his own chronic joint pain and yet despite all the teachings he'd received in all the years of education and the quarts of cortisone injections, he still suffered from tremendous joint pain.

I asked Charles to focus on the worst pain he could muster in his hands and fingers and as he did, we asked Charles' subconscious mind to take us back to the very first scene and the very first situation that had everything to do with the source of the joint pain he had endured for years. His mind took us back to an event when he was five years old. I asked him, "Give me a report of what you are sensing in this moment Charles."

He began to tell me that he was holding his baby brother (who was an infant at the time) and, without meaning to and being a five-year-old, his baby brother began to slip out of his hands until the baby fell and hit the floor.

Tears immediately welt up in his eyes as he felt so terrible as he described the scream his baby brother let out. And to make matters worse, his mother jolted into the room and immediately began to yell at Charles for dropping him.

This became a part of young Charles' perception, seeming to fall short of his mom's expectancy while holding his brother and it was this failed expectancy planted into a developing subconscious mind, that gave him a perception of criticism for making a mistake — and a mistake that needs punished.

Guess where all those swallowed feelings of guilt showed up? His hands.

We released all of the built-up guilt and lathered everything with some serious forgiveness on his part and for his mother, completely shifting that perception.

Over the next few weeks there was some minor reoccurrences in his pain, a clue that there were still some unresolved feelings and lessons to be taken from that moment. Within six weeks' time, chronic pain in his hands that had been there for decades completely disappeared and never returned.

It was here where Charles, a degreed M.D. and professional learned a valuable lesson: when a person has a chronic problem or chronic symptom the only agency that knows the cause and the cure for the problem is the person's subconscious mind.

Look at other places for answers and you're wasting time. Through this focused regression to cause approach, we also learn that as a healer, I don't have to act like I know everything.
In fact, if a doctor, a therapist, or any other degreed professional wants to sabotage their client's appointment, all they have to do is assume that they know exactly where the client needs to go or what they need to do for a healing to take place.

Any variety of symptom is what we use as a guide to the next a level of understanding. The initial sensitizing event of any negative symptom carries a subconscious mission for some form of self-mutilation. That subconscious mission is confirmed and reconfirmed through the additional added sequences of secondary sensitizing events, each one adding more and more mass into that belief and more weight into that perception and more compounding into that program of the initial sensitizing event. Until it gets so heavy, so powerful and so strong that one final subsequent sensitizing event, relatively weak by itself, is equivalent to the "straw that breaks the camel's back" causing *this perception to reach* **critical mass**.

Critical mass is the minimum size or amount of anything required to start a chain reaction.

Now the calling for self-mutilation is so powerful that the subconscious mind's goal achieving agency literally sees its own manifestation of a nasty illness, hijacked immune system or a chronic pain as a goal that *must be successfully achieved.* Anything in the immediate environment is an opportunity, including any microbe, for the subconscious to accomplish its mission.

This is why some people can be exposed to Lyme, have it in their blood, yet never develop the illness. While other people have the lightest brush with a microbe and suddenly develop severe symptoms. It has to do with the subconscious mind's mission and how compounding those SSEs are into that ISE.

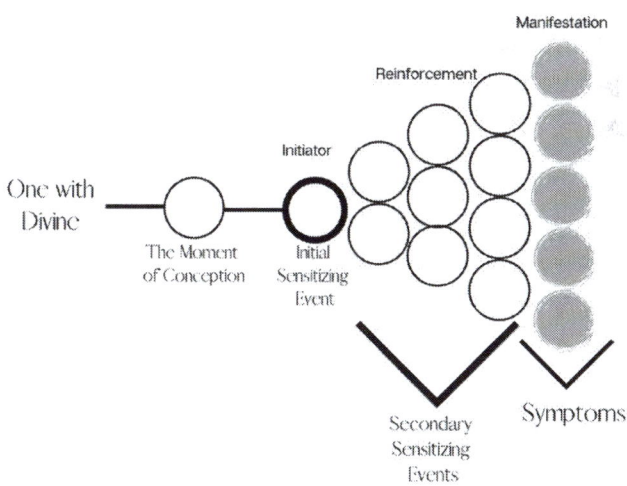

If a patient presents with chronic symptoms and their functional medicine doctor recommends the removal of all processed foods, a parasite cleanse and/or identifies and treats Lyme disease with antibiotics or gives a protocol for virus or recommends an anti-inflammatory diet, deep breathing exercises and other lifestyle modifications yet has no appreciation for that mission of self-mutilation within the subconscious, the symptom will always reappear and this is what we have learned is the basis for reoccurring disorders.

Chronic illness is a chess game between a goal achieving subconscious mind of the patient and a doctor. As you learned about the subconscious mind's ability to achieve whatever it is set on using whatever means necessary (remember the baby chicken and the mechanized robot!) and this is the basis of what causes many doctors to become bewildered, confused and frustrated while their patient becomes more and more hopeless.

What I have witnessed in years of regressing patients to cause shows us that when we examine the cause of chronic illness, what we find is a perfectly functioning goal achieving subconscious mind doing exactly what it's programmed to do.

Remember Sarah's case? Her subconscious mind was programmed, by a seed planting of overhearing her parents discuss her, and it perceived that "I am not supposed to exist." This perception, protected by a critical faculty was what had led her to having difficulty healing even decades later, until she contacted me. This continues to be the most common cause found in the course of my work.

That's the one thing that we must understand. It's the internal congruity or the alignment within us that makes up the vibrational frequencies in our body that summarize the sum total of the signaling our cells are eaves dropping on.

There are aspiring Naturopathic doctors, Functional Medicine doctors, Internist, Integrative Specialist and a variety of different Herbologist and Nutritionist who are convinced that medical science is flawed and that a holistic approach is the appropriate way to obtain healing.

There are many people with chronic symptoms who are looking for a healing themselves and feel the exact same way. All too often these doctors prescribe remedy after remedy as the people chase remedy after remedy hoping that they'll find an outside protocol that will give them the healing they desperately desire.

These people know deep in their hearts that an herb or a nutrient is a much better choice than a medication however the results are inconsistent.

Advancement in achieving long term results is often a battle with repeated backslides and inconsistencies across the board.

Unfortunately, all too often good nutrition, vitamin supplementation, chiropractic adjustments, meditation, massage, acupuncture, body code, emotional code, Reiki, and other forms of alternate and natural health care *become nothing more than natural forms of illness management.*

Dr Vincent Felitti, with over 50 years of experience in childhood trauma, Internal Medicine as well as the recipient of the prestigious Distinguished Worldwide Humanitarian Award had this realization during his time as a physician working with obese patients.

Being a critical thinker and observer, Dr Felitti is also the originator and conductor of the original Adverse Childhood Experiences study. (ACEs)

What the good doctor discovered during the time he operated an obesity clinic, he noticed that with rigorous dietary changes and exercise, they were able to greatly reduce the weight of the obese patients.

The problem was that the patients could not permanently keep the weight from returning. This finding disturbed him enough to inquiry more with his patients about why the weight returned. One of his patients told him, "Don't you get it? We are stuffing down our pain."

This implies that obesity itself is an addiction, related to and stemming from childhood trauma. Until this deep repressed pain or emotional hurt is properly healed, it will reemerge as something else, or in this case as reoccurring weight gain.

Simply stated a Yogi or spiritually enlightened individual can be unaffected by consuming poison and be unharmed by fire.

If your subconscious mind believes that you are protected, engaged with life, fulfilling desires and it is fully impressed with the idea that your body operates and functions as one with Divine, you can withstand far more exposures than what conventional, mainstream science tells us. Having a sense of purpose rather than feeling like a victim tremendously impacts how your cells function and even how you age. (28)

Remember, mainstream science teaches us that we are mechanistic, machines that have limitations.

In the Southern part of United States, there is a religious group known as the Baptist fundamentalist. Amongst this organization are members who have developed the mindset to place themselves into a state of religious ecstasy, where they believe that God protects them.

To demonstrate this, they work with several venomous snakes including copperheads and rattlesnakes. Occasionally, they will even get bitten by the snake without being affected by the snake's venom. (29)

Additionally, some of them will go as far as drinking high levels of strychnine, a highly toxic alkaloid, during this state of belief and it has no effect on them.

On June 15, 2005, Amanda Dennison from Alberta, Canada accomplished a feat that was recorded in the *Guinness Book of World Records* for achieving the longest recorded fire walk on Earth. She was able to walk two hundred and twenty feet along red-hot coals that averaged 1700°F without a single injury on her feet.

How could these people achieve such supernatural feats? It is because of their beliefs. Imagine if we believed we were Divine beings and capable of doing whatever we wanted, achieving our greatest dream, healing from chronic states of disease and living a fulfilling life of abundance and happiness. The quantum field acts like a giant mirror.

All of this is available to us as the quantum model of the universe has no limitations. It is us through our painful experiences and hurts, especially during our childhood years, that originate the limitations we carry.

On a regular basis, I have patients who eat organic food, use muscle testing for the best supplement choice possible, drink the cleanest water, take all necessary precautions to live a toxic free life and still contact me with any varying degree of unresponsive symptoms and ongoing chronic reoccurring conditions. Why?

Because in their deepest part of their subconscious mind, there is a memory from a circumstance with unresolved issues that are calling for self-mutilation.

The body of evidence that confirms these kinds of situations only continues to expand. Some involve leading edge researchers who suggest that unresolved negative emotions have the capacity to create the physical conditions that we recognize as chronic illness. A mind body interaction was carefully documented in a landmark study at Duke University by James Blumenthal. His work recognized that long held emotions such as disappointment, resentment, anger, anxiety, fear and frustration we're directly responsible for creating tension, inflammation, high blood pressure and clogged arteries-contributors to the greatest threat to the life of adults over 65: heart disease. (30)

Achieving a state of health and harmony are only done with the right mindset on all levels. A person can eat as healthy as they would wish, yet if there's a subconscious program operating for self-mutilation or self-punishment, there won't be enough organically grown vegetables on the planet to shift this person into a complete state of healing.

Likewise, there are people who smoke, drink, eat pasta, love cheeseburgers and pepperoni pizza and yet live to be 100 years old because their life is so full of love vitality and purpose that they are thankful for every moment they are alive and therefore their body responds with longevity.

A life supporting set of early sensitizing events easily explains the individual who smokes 3 packs of cigarettes a day, is 78 years old and still as healthy as an ox! These sensitizing events compounded by secondary sensitizing events protected by a critical faculty can kill the healthiest eater and equally keep the cigarette smoking hamburger fanatic alive and thriving. This is the underlying mechanism of how a doctor can cut out a tumor yet consistently the person develops another growth.

This is how it works through all walks of life for every person. Virtually everything that happens to us later in our adult life begins as a coping mechanism in childhood. And it is important to point out that it is not a matter of blaming people. These patterns are completely unconscious and nobody's aware of it. Nobody decides to be this way. Where does it originate from? Well for that, you must go back to childhood in nearly every single case.

Oftentimes, people can perceive themselves as being blamed even when they're not being blamed. Dr Christine Northrup, a well-known physician and best-selling author once said that there is kind of conspiracy between the doctor and the patient. It revolves around this unspoken idea not to talk about uncomfortable, personal circumstances about the patient's life and for the doctor it's much simpler and faster to hand out the pills. It is also easier for the patient as it avoids any chance of bringing up uncomfortable inquiries.

Moreover, some people do not want to release their diseases. Perhaps this stems from the mechanistic model that implies that our actions do not really matter. It could also be that some people have what is commonly referred to as **secondary gain**.

This means that having the symptoms, illness or pathology gives the person something they view as more beneficial then if they were to have possess a full bill of health. For example, when a child only gets direct attention from their parents when they are sick, to a child's brain, they learn that "if I am sick, I am lovable" or "I only get attention when I am feeling ill" so they rationalize that feeling ill is the better choice and they identify with their illness. These become the adults who, almost as a badge of honor, tell you their name when first meeting them and then tell you their list of diagnosis.

In fact, it has been said that only 30% of people who go to doctors, take the appropriate steps, and obey any instructions that they are given. A good majority of people go to doctors, not necessarily to cure their illness, but to have some relief from their acute symptoms.

Another barrier to healing, I believe, is an emotional barrier and I think on the part of physicians themselves. Many doctors have not yet properly dealt with their own pain, their own stressors, and their own traumas. This shows up in the high rate of suicide, depression, and burnout amongst doctors.

When we are born into the world our parents make up a majority of that early environment and no matter what their conscious intentions are parents cannot pass on to us what they themselves do not have.

I believe we are all victims of victims and not to pass blame on anyone, but this is how the psyche of our mind, which is a *reality maker*, all begins from in each of us.

If two loved starved people come together and form a child, as much as they hope, wish and intend to shower that child with love--the stuff they did not receive when they were a child — (and if they haven't healed their own trauma) -- they end up giving that child what they themselves were subjected to when they were that age.

It happens to all human beings alike no matter the race, background, or ethnicity, whether they are a farmer, a goldminer, or a celebrity.

In our society parents are often taught to ignore the infant until they cry for attention. First, we checked their diaper. After ensuring the infant has a clean diaper, the conditioning most of us fall into is we give the child a bottle or a blanket, assuming that's what they need.

In reality, it is connection they need, but essential human needs are not understood in our modern society and chances are the infant child does not receive the connection they need.

Giving the child a bottle or a blanket and having this need not met the child often continues to cry so the parent gets more and more fed up sometimes mumbling the words, "Stop crying! You are driving me crazy!" The child's mind is equivalent to a patch of very fertile soil growing whatever seeds are planted in it with no questions asked.

This kind of rhetoric is misunderstood and carelessly used by people along all walks of life, no matter the level of fame.

Arnold Schwarzenegger was being interviewed during the release of his film "True Lies." He said he would never let his three-year old watch any of his movies. His follow up comment however, solidified this carelessness and ignorance of the young an impressionable mind. "My nine-month-old, she doesn't care what's on the TV!"

Ouch.

My hope is that you get this concept and understand what potentially adverse experiences will someday be lived out as adults, if the concept is never respected for their young minds and how they form.

Now, like Arnold's ignorance, mom's faulty assumption at this time that her child doesn't yet have a functional vocabulary, so she assumes the child doesn't know what mommy means when she says, "you're driving me crazy." The problem is that those words are recorded in the subconscious mind of the child, and they become a part of that child's perception of who they are.

The parent(s) continue to criticize the child for their inconvenience as if this kind of parent wants the child to somehow just figure life out and become naturally good at it. During these moments if a child ever falls short of this expectancy, like in our case with Dr Charles, they get punished and criticized for making a mistake. This becomes a significant overlooked and misunderstood problem.

As developing humans, we don't learn through our successes; we learn from our mistakes, and we do so by trial and error.

This is part of the normal developing process we all have and go through as children. If the child knocks over a glass of juice and the parent treats the event as something to be scolded by and punished for, rather than a simple mistake to be learned from, the dreadful **Curse of Perfectionism** begins to sprout in their subconscious. The curse of perfectionism is a perception when a child naturally has a can-do attitude and nature, yet they hear the words, "You are driving me crazy" and begins to ponder that "My mom and daddy aren't happy now but I can make them happier. I can do better. I can please them. I can make them happy."

However, the problem is that the anger coming from mom or dad towards their child has *nothing* to do with the child. It only broadcasts the unresolved pain, unhealed trauma, and the suffering that is still present within the parents. If those parents have unresolved traumas, and they are programmed to criticize from their own childhood experiences, it doesn't matter how perfect the child's performance is, the parents will still only seek and find some area to criticize because that's what their own perception and programming is capable of viewing. In fact, they will *only* see through the lens of imperfection even if the child's own performance was mere millimeters away from perfection.

So, as the parents, obedient to their own subconscious programs, criticize the child, the child's perception is of one that assumes, "Well, I try to do better and they are still upset. They still yell. They are still angry. They are still unhappy. Well, I can do even better, and I can make them happy."

But remember the child still learns through the process of trial and error and as that trial occurs once again the child makes an error, and the programmed parent criticizes and yells again.

That positive can-do attitude that resides in the child as now a bit weaker with each compounding criticism, yet the child still insists, "I can do better. I can do better! There must be a way I can make mom and dad happy! I can do better!" The child tries to do their best over and over repeatedly.

However, whatever that best is, is met against the parents' own programs which are still operating to seek and find something to criticize.

That criticism the child hears is absorbed and compounds with every additional criticism eventually leading to the subconscious mind of the child to build a perception of, "I must be really awful. I tried my best and my hardest to do good and nothing's good enough."

That exhausted attitude of can do, is now so weak and desperate looking for a way to please mom and dad. Remember, no matter what the child does they cannot succeed because they cannot be perfect in the eyes of a parent who is programmed to be critical. As this pattern repeats itself during the first five years of life until one day the child's exhausted mind finally concludes the notion that, "Maybe if I'm perfect, mom and dad can't yell at me anymore."

At this moment the child has now officially been subconsciously programmed to perceive something that is an *impossibility* to achieve. There can be no perfection viewed through their own self-image as he or she has been trained to only seek out the negative traits, qualities, and attributes within themselves. In other words, they will only look for the bad within themself.

Recall the observer effect? The act of looking for something creates the very thing you're looking for. So, as the child matures, they will only seek the bad, the failures and negativity within themselves and they will always find it. It will always be created as that is aligned with their beliefs.

Finding the bad, the failures and the negative will only intensify the program calling for punishment to kick into higher gear. As you can imagine, this is the beginning of the end.
As this child goes through life they will naturally focus on the parts of their life and only view theses as failures and inadequacies which leads to more criticism quickly following. This directly causes any feelings of self-worth to only diminish.

Recall the law of compounding? When I said this is the beginning of the end, I am expressing that this pattern often leads to chronic illness because the mental is the causative factor, the mind creates reality, and we are all reality makers.

As life experiences confirm these inner callings and they grow continually stronger and stronger for self-punishment, self-mutilation, over time, that calling will only grow stronger.
It's because of this compounding that the mind will not be satisfied next year with the tools that it's using to inflict self-punishment in the present year. The natural state of progression shows us that total self-destruction is the ultimate form of self-punishment. Chronic illness, autoimmune, and cancer are certainly tools for the subconscious mind's goal achieving agency that is programmed for self-destruction.

Does this mean that all who are in a scenario similar to this nine-month-old are traumatized? Not necessarily. Some people may believe that a disturbing news story or a particular movie "traumatized" them after viewing it.

Although understandable, but it's a misinterpretation on the impact that trauma does. Although stressful, it was not necessarily a traumatic event. Peter Levine once said, "All traumatic events are stressful but not all stressful events are necessarily traumatic."

In this way we can also point out that for a trauma to occur we must examine the sensitivity and the perception of the individual. I have worked with identical twins throughout the years who came to me with various symptoms.

Genetically these people are the same, yet, in one case, one of them exhibits much higher levels of chronic inflammation, ongoing digestive disturbances, autoimmune markers on lab testing and a higher vulnerability to various microbes (virus and parasites) when compared to the other twin. How could this be? During their infancy, one of them was held and welcomed in the presence of the parent much more than the other one.

Now review these two brief paragraphs again from published articles in Pediatrics, the official journal of the American Academy of Pediatrics.

*The architecture of the brain is constructed through an ongoing process that begins before birth and continues into adulthood and establishes either a sturdy or a fragile foundation for **all** health, learning and behavior that follows.*

The interaction of genes and experiences literally shapes the circuitry of the developing brain and is critically influenced by mutual responsiveness of adult child relationships particularly in the early childhood years.

Trauma occurs if an individual is constricted from their original self, compressed on the inside and left diminished *after the event*, and this constriction persists throughout the person's entire life.

Suzanne Sommers, the popular American actress and author from the television show *Three's Company*, was an example of someone who underwent several various natural methods for curing her health struggles, including a diagnosis of breast cancer in 2000.

She authored several books promoting alternate treatments for cancer, including Knockout, where she interviews various doctors that are focused on reversing cancer. She emphasized nutrition, healthy lifestyle changes, avoiding toxins and dietary supplementations with therapies that build up the body's immune system.

Despite all these positive changes, there was something deeper still operating that was unaddressed. For decades, she fought with breast cancer until she succumbed to it in 2023 as it had spread to other body parts, including her brain, and lead to multiple complications.

In her book, *Keeping Secrets*, she indicated she had grown up with an alcoholic father who was abusive and tormented her in her earliest years.

In her own words, she points out those early perceptions by describing her encounters with her father. "I remember being berated over and over again as a child…'You're nothing, You're stupid, You're hopeless, you're worthless, You're a piece of crap' and I believed it." Such early childhood impressions take a lasting toll.

Even clean food, healthy living and regular use of supplements has no chance against a subconscious mind set on self-mutilation.

CHAPTER 7

The Greatest Part of Me is Something You Do Not See: We are Non-Physical Beings

There is no problem outside of you that is superior to the power within you.- Bob Proctor

Most doctors, healers, therapists of various kinds and all manner of internists are all striving for the same goal: to assist in any way to help their patients and their clients maximize their own body's ability to heal.

However, this can get into a gray area when it comes to working with the mind and body and the psychosomatic approach for healing because this is a hotbed for experimentation.

Although modalities like hypnosis have been studied, even extensively by the United States army and the CIA, implementing these practices into a therapeutic approach it is still in its infancy. There are many reasons for that and oftentimes it has more to do with the individual healer and their intention along with the interaction with their client then it may do with the specific technique.

For example, if a doctor seeing his patient is only interested in the financial gain he or she has to benefit from the interaction with the patient, healing may be very limited.

Remember we talked about vibration and Renee Peoc'h's experiment? Well, a human being's mirror neurons can pick up very quickly if the doctor or therapist they're working with is doing it for the right reason or just for financial gain.

So, trust your instincts when working with any practitioner and trust your gut feelings as they don't lie, even if your conscious lying rational mind does.

Looking at all the evidence. It's clear that some experiments fail while some succeed and others like hypnosis EMDR, EFT, dialectal behavior therapy, and Holographic Manipulation Therapy® all can take potentially decades to be integrated into mainstream not to mention that mainstream research generally favors methods that are more well known then ones that may be up and coming.

Look at the example of how long it took penicillin to be fully accepted as an antibiotic approach. Alexander Fleming discovered it in 1928, yet it took until 1965 before it was fully integrated as an approach main mainstream for anti-microbial properties.

I want to make it clear that when I discuss the body's ability to repair itself, I am in no way suggesting that we should just forgo any kind of medicine or care that you are currently having with the physician because embarking on anything new should always be done with the permission of a general care practitioner and in no way is this a substitute for potentially any medications that you may currently be taking.

If you are in doubt or unsure always error on the side of caution and ask your doctor before starting anything new.

Now, let's introduce you to the non-physical side of yourself. This will be a vitally important concept to understand when we begin the techniques.

The institute of Heart Math has achieved several fascinating discoveries involving the human nervous system. One of the most exciting discoveries is the successful measuring of a field of electromagnetic energy that permeates from our heart.

This field is measurable by instruments anywhere from 3 to 8 feet in diameter and it surrounds our entire body. Note: When asked, these scientists stated that the size of this field was only observed to be 3 to 8 feet because of the limitations of their current equipment, implying that this field is actually much larger!

Known as a **torus field,** it originates from the human heart. In fact, there is compelling evidence that suggest that the physical heart is coupled to a field of information that is not bound to the classical limits of time and space. (31) This finding is one of our keys to understanding how we can create enormous shifts when we begin to work with our holographic memories and clear out past imprints of trauma.

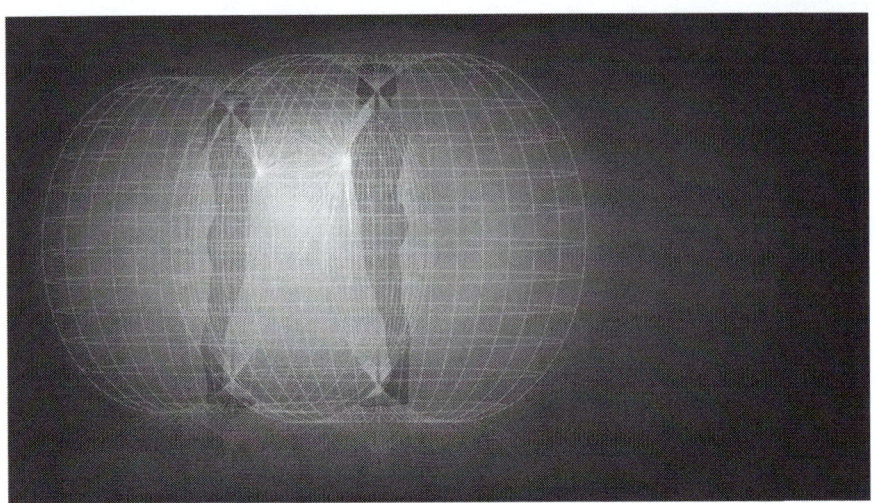

The human heart has its own nervous system and its own *brain*. Discovered and verified in 1991, there are approximately 40,000 **sensory neurites**, which are a group of specialized brain-like cells that are found in the heart. Similar to the functions of the brain, these neurites can *feel*, *remember* and *even think*. What is even more intriguing is that they seem to be able to do these functions completely independent of the brain. (32)

The electromagnetic field permeates and emanates emotional data all around us and as we will soon learn, it is far more than this. So, as people move through the world, we are constantly entraining with others around us.

We do this without even knowing it, but we have all seen this work. Imagine that you are at your home and working in your kitchen just thinking about the day and slicing up an apple.

Suddenly, a family member walks in behind you and without you looking at their face or reading their body language, you can automatically *feel* if they are in a bad mood.

The International Peace Project study conducted in the Middle East was published in the Journal of Conflict Resolution and shows a larger picture of this connection between people.

The study documented the effects that occurred on particular days of the month during specific moments, when various people who were conditioned to go into a meditative state and resonate the feeling of peace within their body. They did this as they were positioned throughout different areas which were significantly damaged from wars in the Middle East.

During that moment when these trained subjects went into the feeling of peace in their heart and resonating this throughout their torus field, the activities of terrorists stopped. Along with this crimes and emergency room visits and even traffic accidents all dropped. These findings demonstrate that a small group of people who achieved peace within themselves reflected this peace in the world around them.

Imagine the implications here. Healing yourself on one end and changing your state of mind will impact others around you in positive ways, including your children.

The next chapter will begin the process of accessing this, but first we need to understand what it is we are interacting with. When you fully grasp this, you will have the key to have volitional control over your entire neurology.

When we think about the torus field, there is a concept we refer to as the holographic nervous system. Part of this electromagnetic field is another aspect we call the proprioceptive grid. It is linked to our proprioceptive nervous system.

Our minds are not just limited by our brain, nor is it limited to our physical body. Thought energy is able to reach out and interact with other people, plants and animals. We read that in previous examples before and we learned that it is not just something limited to humans.

Jim Corbett, one of the most famous and prolific hunters ever known, described this sensation while he was hunting a man-eating tiger in the Kumaon region in India. In his book, *Man-eaters of Kumaon*, he wrote about his experiences during the time he was recruited by the government to stop the killings of people that these tigers were responsible for.

On multiple occasions, he mentions that his life had been saved by *feeling* the glare from a hidden tiger as it was stalking him in the jungle. It caused the hair on the back of his neck stand up as he felt the gaze from the tiger's presence, and this led to him changing his direction and ultimately escape the awaiting ambush.

Understand that this phenomenon is very common in people as indicated by surveys.

Approximately 95% of the population have experienced this strange sensation that occurs when they were been stared at. (33) Perhaps you can recall a time when you felt as though as you were being watched only to turn around and find someone looking right at you. It can be described as an unnerving and petrified sensation yet is more common than most people may recognize.

So, where does this feeling come from? Because your body interprets the contours of thought energy as pressure *pushing on the proprioceptive grid.*

Have you ever had the experience when you are driving a car, and something tells you to look in your mirror? Then you look in your side mirror and you look in your rear-view mirror glancing around to see if something is behind you. Yet, you don't see anything, but deep down you know someone, or something is there.

You can feel the pressure, as if something is there. Then suddenly, someone appears! A person you did not see in your mirrors walks by. How did that happen? You *sensed* someone without seeing them?
In that moment, your subconscious mind, being a protective mind, gave you signals. It took your field of proprioceptive spatial awareness and extended it to include the car. The same thing has happened to women who have had the experience of being in a club or a bar somewhere.

Next, someone with less than savory intentions begin to fix their gaze upon them. If this or something similar has occurred to you, you can recall how that felt. It started as pressure on your torus field, and then following that was subtle icky feeling. How do you explain this?

Intention, or creating a precise thought, causes pressure that is interpreted by your proprioceptive nervous system, your mirror neurons and your subconscious mind communicates it to you in the only language it knows how to: *sensation.*

Everything you experience from the outside world is mediated through your proprioceptive neurology. It simultaneously interacts with the heart's nervous system and with your **mirror neurons.**
Mirror neurons are a distinctive class of nerve cells that are capable of being stimulated when an individual executes a motor response with skeletal muscle as well as when the individual observes another individual performing a same or similar act. This is the part of you that goes active creating a fear response including the increased heart rate, rapid breathing, adrenaline release and increase in sweat while watching gruesome scene in a horror movie.

All this internal interaction creates a field of awareness within the torus shape that surrounds you. It behaves like both a sensing mechanism, or membrane, as well as functioning as a filing system for your informational data. (33) This includes all your past experiences and traumatic memories.

This is the reason behind people moving their hands while they are talking. If you notice, it is common occurrence that a person will move their hands in specific ways and to various locations around their body with gestures as they discuss something. If they talk about the same thing over and over, unconsciously their hands tend to move to the same places over and over again.

This is because they're accessing the encoded information within their torus field both interoceptively and exteroceptively at the same time.

The system of your neurology that governs all of this is known as your **proprioceptive nervous system,** or PNS. The proprioceptive nervous system is most commonly recognized as the governing systems that gives your brain feedback in your position in space, but it is much more than that.

Think of it as sort of a sixth sense, but it wouldn't be limited to just your 6th sense because there are at least six different channels of neurological feedback that your proprioceptive neurology monitors. It would be more accurately described as your sixth, seventh, eighth, ninth, tenth, and eleventh sense.

These senses include time and spatial relationships around our body.

This is commonly what is known and accounts for the ability to close your eyes and with your hands reach out and touch your nose with your finger. Or tasks like walking without watching the activity of your feet.
Other areas include exteroception, or interpretations of data outside of the body. These include thermoreception or sensation of heat and cold. Nociception, which is the ability to perceive painful sensations, mechanoreception, which gives sensation relation to our joint functions, and even electromagnetic fields. Along with exteroception, our PNS has another channel called interception.

Interoception is the awareness of the feelings and the movement inside of the body. This is important to understand because the vast majority of body feelings that we experience are subconscious: they are actually taking place below the threshold of conscious awareness.

For instance, your body is composed of nearly 70% water. Have you ever carried a bucket full of water and attempt to walk with it? What happens to the water?

The water inside of the bucket sloshes all around as it moves. Well, being that we are approximately 70% water, this means that we too slosh when we move around.

Why don't we feel it? It is because your proprioceptive nervous system is filtering out a tremendous amount of those sensations so we are not aware of them.
These feelings of water moving around are present when we walk, but we are not aware of them. So, when we begin to build up emotional energies and we start to build up emotional experiences or emotional encoded thought forms within our body, these are also lodged in our proprioceptive system, and they too will generate subconscious body feelings. We often don't pay attention to them (yet) until they become so strong that they break that threshold of preconscious awareness and now we're forced to take care of them in some way.

Emotions are generated this way. Every emotion that you have starts off as an interoceptive sensation and then your neurology looks at the context, the situation and it does systems check to find out if it's ever had that feeling in that context before. If it finds a match it opens that holographic "file" and it applies those labels to the new body feeling and now you've got a name for your feeling.

If you're one of those people gifted with empathy on overdrive, one of the fastest ways that you can disconnect from body states is the moment you become aware of a body state, ask yourself one simple question.

"Is this mine?"
You'll instantly create an energetic disconnect between you and the source of that information. (Remember, we are picking up on people's thoughts and emotional energy around us all the time)

Now if the information is coming from within your own field the next question you would ask is "What else could this be?" The simple act of asking that question disconnects that interoceptive sensation that you have from the label you've neurologically assigned to it, and it gives you the option of assigning a different meaning to the body feeling.

One of these channels is electromagnetic fields, which is what Heart Math Institute successfully measured.

Skeptics may suggest these are the result of an illusion or the result of subtle clues like a slight shadow or noise in the background.

Reading about how a hunter senses a tiger staring at him and discussing women being gawked at in a bar is one thing, but a study published in *the Journal of Neuroscience* flirts with the incredible.

Researchers investigated whether the brain could detect or "see" another person's behaviors even when the ability of visual sight was not possible.

Cortical blindness refers to a loss of vision that occurs when the primary visual cortex of the eye is no longer functional typically associated with an injury.

The ability to visually perceive the world through the sense of the eye is no longer achievable even if the eye is still technically sound but this study shows the brain is still able to perceive visual data.

In the study a patient's brain was shown to still react from another person's gaze even if they could not see them staring at them. Using a brain scan the patient was exposed to gazes directly at him and gazes directed away from him.

Visually speaking, nothing should have occurred because his visual sensory system could not perceive when the person was staring at them and when they weren't. But the brain scan indicated that parts of his brain reacted when he was directly looked at.

Perhaps you may have noticed that you can be asleep and, somehow, you "know" when somebody comes home, even without hearing them? You can *feel* it in the house.
Have you ever noticed that houses that don't have people in them breakdown and decay faster than houses with families inside of them? Houses that have no occupants living within them deteriorate faster than houses with people living in them, even if they do nothing to fix or maintain the house! Why? Because the energetic torus field, an energy that human beings give off, that has a negative entropic effect.

In other words, you are consciousness; a source of light and energy constantly moving from disorganization to organization. Now, when a family of people inhabit a house, their combined proprioceptive neurology expands to include the house, just like in the car example earlier.

We all share to a deeper connection with the world around us that is beyond the physical world and what we've been led to believe. Although this may be considered an area of taboo that is not taken seriously by mainstream science, there are a group of well accomplished scientists that have designed experiments to explore this non-physical world deeper.

A pioneer in these studies is biologist Rupert Sheldrake PhD. Many of the scientific experiments he has conducted have indicated that people indeed guess far above chance as to whether they were being watched by another person.

Psychologist William Braud PhD as well as anthropologist Marilyn Schlitz PhD also found substantial evidence of the sense of being stared with their experiments using closed circuit TV.

Using randomized controlled trials and placing people at two distinct locations, the experiment consisted of one person who would focus intently on the distant person's image without any ordinary way of knowing, and time and time again, the results suggested that people were sensitive and able to detect another person's attention being focused on them.

Additionally, these studies also tracked emotional responses by measuring changes in the body through skin conductance. Strikingly, the autonomic activity in the body was shown to increase during the moment when a person was being *remotely observed*.

Dean Radin PhD, a psychologist at the Institute of Noetic Sciences reported further positive evidence of increased brain activity measured on an Electroencephalograph while being observed or stared at by another person.

He also used caution and great consideration to exclude any and all possible outside factors as well as tightly controlled conditions and still produced positive results of this phenomena. A meta-analysis published in 2005 closer examined a significant number of studies and concluded that a very precise, yet repeatable effect had been demonstrated with odds against chance ranging from 62 to 1 to 1000 to 1.

Let us look at this scientific data in another way. You are probably aware that a large amount of people take aspirin as a daily preventative to heart attacks, as it has an effect of thinning the blood.

From the statics, the effect size is incredibly small at 0.03%, but this is still real enough for Bayer aspirin to get approval from the FDA for marketing on the side of their bottles that "aspirin can reduce the risk of death if taken as directed by a doctor as soon as a heart attack is suspected." This marketing strategy operates on the basis of really small effect sizes, but at 0.03%, is a real effect.

Now, when you look at the effect of telepathy experiments, the effect is 0.16%, which is five times greater.[34]

In other words, telepathy is *five times* more scientifically verifiable then aspirin preventing a heart attack but almost everyone accepts that idea about aspirin and associated prevention of heart attacks while at the same time people have trouble believing that telepathy could be a real phenomenon.

It's not woo-woo or fantasy. This is the research.

Now that you have an better idea of your non-physical self along with a better understanding that your mind is linked to a field outside of your physical body, it is time to show you how to begin the process of interacting with it, the same as you would with a computer or an iPhone, and furthermore, changing how certain experiences, such as overwhelming emotional pain or trauma, has been coded into your mind and body.

To do this, we need to ensure that the next chapter is understood fully and completely. For best results, read it repeatedly. This is where things get really interesting!

CHAPTER 8

Procedures for accessing our Holographic Dashboard

"You are like a captain navigating a ship. You must give the right orders, thoughts and images to your subconscious which controls and governs all your experiences." – **Joseph Murphy**

We all have tremendous control over our own neurology in incredible ways once we know how to access the dashboard that controls it. A significant majority of people simply do not understand that the imagination, a key part in the subconscious mind as well the conscious mind needs to work together to do this properly and effectively.

Unlike hypnosis, which bypasses the critical faculty, we will be introducing a technology known as **Holographic Manipulation Therapy®** which incorporates *all areas* of the mind, including the critical faculty, in this process.

This creates a much more powerful and deeper change. As we begin this chapter, it is important to remember that powerful stuff is always the simplest. More complicated applications can be very powerful, but they are almost always more specialized and therefore only good in specific scenarios or circumstances.

Imagination and visualizing play a key role in these techniques. It's not just fantasy although fantasizing does contribute to this, yet the overall mediator is connecting and linking them to the physical body. So, we must use the physical body, as it is a significant part of the accessing the subconscious mind. In fact, more accurately said is that your body is your subconscious mind (35).

Furthermore, we must follow the rules of how we can access this part of us. Once you are *beyond* the use of your five senses and you begin to pay attention to the energy and the quantum field, your higher mind is connecting to much higher levels of frequency and therefore higher levels of information.

The coding of the structure that governs and manages all these different vibrational levels of you and how you manage experiences and assign meaning to each one is accessible to you, if you can do three things: The first one is to *be playful*.

Now, I understand that each person has their own personality and sets of behaviors that they live by on a routine. The reason that playfulness is necessary is because of the simple frequency of physics.

Being playful, using your imagination and pretending automatically sets the tone of your mind at a much higher frequency then being serious and skeptical. By skeptical, I don't mean being a little uneasy or uncertain about this process, especially if you've never done anything like this before.

The skeptical I am referring to is already having a predetermined perception of that this is not going to work, therefore you've already set yourself up for failure.

Moreover, I won't ask you to believe any of this. That's right. I will not ask that you believe this or try to trust in it moving forward.

What I will ask is that you don't actively fight or resist the process. If you are fully engaged, and the key word is (I already mentioned) to _play pretend_, you will be able to change anything you want. Remember the early chapter on bucket-listing? It is vitally important to start with that as you incorporate this into a routine.

Playing pretend, and just acting like you are participating in the process automatically places you on a higher frequency of thinking and it is this exact process that will help you override lower frequencies.

How? Because from a physics standpoint, higher frequencies always dominate lower frequencies.

So, play pretend!

The second thing that is necessary is to _become absorbed and focused_ on what you're doing. Imagine a red balloon that is floating right out in front of you. Using your hand reach out and playfully poke it with your finger. Because of the holographic nature of our memories and PNS working together, you can practically _feel_ the elastic, gentle push, and the flexing back it does to it's original form mimicking the wall of a balloon as you poke the side of it?

Now image rubbing your thumb across the surface of the rubbery side and *feel* the slight tension building. Listen to that annoying, squeaky sound that is associated with rubbing a balloons wall. See? You can practically feel the balloon and hear that sound as you are pretending to touch it. Now, take a smell of that balloon and you suddenly notice a smell of latex comes into your awareness. This is just a simple example of what I am referring to by being focused and absorbed in the process.

Another example of being focused and absorbed is to imagine you are holding a fresh, beautiful lemon in your hand. Observe it with your eyes and notice the bright yellow color and the tiny pores all over it. Gently squeeze it and notice the texture it has against your hand. Now, imagine that you have a small knife in the other hand, and you gently and carefully slice into the side of the lemon, and you notice that little citrusy burst of mist and the instant smell of lemon. If you are fully absorbed and focused with your mind on this imaginary lemon, you will almost certainly have noticed you are producing more saliva.

This simple demonstration of imaging something, or visualizing, with focus and absorption bridges your senses so they seem to interact with this imaginary picture. The human mind behaves like a hologram which attunes itself to the universal hologram (33). All your five senses work this way. All your memories, especially the most powerful and influential ones from conception to age 5, have the traits and characteristics of holograms because of the methodical organization of storing a tremendous amount of data, information, with varying frequency and amplitude, all within the electrostatic field the comprises the human mind.

All this data is directly related to the torus field that we learned about. Think of your torus field as a storage and retrieval system, with the ability to immediately revive anything you ask for that has been stored. Consider the red balloon example.

When I had you imagine a balloon and a lemon, an image immediately popped up in front of you. The location it popped up was what we refer to as the **Holographic Dashboard**.

It is the frontal, anterior plane of your torus field that literally acts like a *virtual reality computer* screen to your subconscious mind. Within this screen, occupies all information which influences how you view and assign meaning to your reality.

Everything within your permanent memory, to some extent, is stored here and therefore is also subject to recall, even if your conscious mind has difficulty understanding what exactly "it" is. It does not matter. The data is still present in some location in front of you.

Refer to the images. Anything in the frontal plane, that is inside of your torus field is, for all practical purposes, is an operational and functional piece of data that your subconscious mind interprets as a factual solid object.

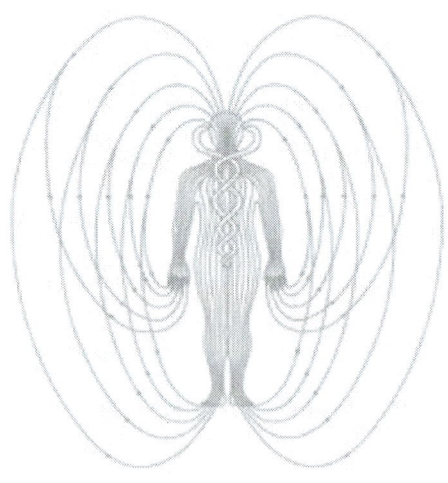

The technique of **Holographic Deletion**, which is coming up next, instructs that you use your physical body to point where you feel the unpleasant body feeling and reach out with your other hand to touch the image floating in your holographic dashboard.

This process creates a *somatic bridge*. A somatic bridge is the process of using your body, engaging all parts of the mind model (the conscious, subconscious, and the critical faculty), your proprioceptive nervous system and connecting all of the interoception (body feelings) and exterior reception (arm and fingers) and connecting the entire *internal* holographic component with the entire *external* holographic component and creating multiple routes to the same information. This process generates tremendous recruitment of all the various channels of your neurology for creating tremendous change very quickly.

By engaging and utilizing the body, (as opposed to sitting quietly like in hypnosis or meditation) including the eyes and the hands (that take up significant real estate on the brain) it activates the right and left neural hemispheres and all different channels of neural circuits.

Remember, it is these circuits that are bound to the same areas of the brain work on all the different areas. That is the reason that Tylenol is shown to help alleviate the pain associated with a breakup[36].

In other words, look at the quote from Dr Gabor Mate: ..."physical pain and emotional pain; the suffering is experienced the same part of the brain. So, when people suffer emotional rejection the same part of the brain will light up as if you stuck them with a knife."

These techniques will be using *all* parts of your neurology to create powerful shifts in your perception. Somatic bridging, or the active process of pointing where you feel it activates the external construct, which is your arm and pointer finger governed by your central nervous system and skeletal muscle and the act of pointing to the feeling, connects it to your internal proprioceptive nervous system where the body feeling is located.

All these different areas involved recruit more of the neurology engaged and, in the process, we're bringing more resources to bear on the situation. As you will soon see, that's why change happens, and it happens so fast.

As Marilyn Ferguson, editor of the Brain Mind Bulletin points out, "A feature of a hologram is its efficiency. Billions of bits of information can be stored in a tiny space the pattern of the holographic imprint."

So, the emphasis of being focused and absorbed is key to accessing the data that is contained in a holographic like structure and once we access it, we can change it.

The third thing that is necessary is to *follow the simple instructions*. This includes the step-by-step process we will cover next as well as beginning with your bucket-list that was covered in the beginning of this book.

For practical purposes, follow the order of these instructions and doing it in this order, especially when you are just beginning the process.

Before starting the technique, we must also understand how the subconscious mind is going to respond to us when we are attempting to communicate with it. Reading and learning this list is essential for moving forward and having success in using the techniques. Write these down and commence these to your memory.

The subconscious mind *always answers first*. Deepak Chopra MD once said that whenever you ask your subconscious mind a question, it will answer within three seconds, but it usually does not answer in any kind of verbalization. However, it will always answer first.

Earlier I asked you to imagine a red balloon. Did you notice how quickly one came to your mind? If I asked you to think of a green balloon, observe how quickly one appears right in front of you in your holographic dashboard. Think of your home now. Think of your living room.

Think of your vehicle. Notice how quickly your mind retrieves whatever it is you ask for and displays it on the screen of space right in front of you? Your subconscious mind will always answer, and it will always answer first.

Secondly, as you have already noticed, is that *it always answers correctly*. Your subconscious mind always answers correctly and accurately and has no ability to lie to you. After you ask it a question it only responds by retrieving the answer quickly and accurately.

When you were asked to imagine a red balloon, for example, your mind answered first, and it answered correctly by reviving its perception of a red balloon. It did not show you a red kite or a red firetruck, right? It immediately retrieved and displayed a red balloon directly in front of you.

These points are very important to understand because as you begin the process of asking your subconscious questions, there will almost reach a moment when you *think you are making it up*, as *it won't make logical sense* to you. (you are not dealing with a logical mind-that is the conscious mind)

So, let's do a brief review to understand these important steps on how to correctly dialogue with your subconscious mind and the holographic dashboard that surrounds your body in a torus field.

Rules:
1. Be playful.
2. Be focused and absorbed.
3. Follow each step.

Your subconscious mind always answers first, it answers honestly, truthfully, and accurately, and you may think that you're making it up and have an urge to want to edit those answers. Memorize these traits before moving forward with the exercise to completely dissolve away any resistance from your critical faculty and to ensure you are accessing the areas that will provide you with the most change.

From the last chapters we learned that we are non-physical beings. We also learned that there is a field around us that act both a protective mechanism, a sensing mechanism and an information storage and retrieval processing mechanism.

In order to change a part of ourselves that we do not like, a part that is from a perception stored in a holographic container, we do not need to know where it originated from or the circumstances that caused it: We only need to access a fragment of the holographic data in order to change it, so let's get started with the procedures and techniques for deep healing to occur.

Anchoring into Safety

Before we begin to work on reversing the holographic imprinted data that our subconscious mind interprets as currently active and operating, which leads to symptoms such as anxiety, panic, flashbacks and others symptoms related to post traumatic stress disorder, we first need to establish safety into our subconscious mind.

We do this by anchoring certain frequencies, along with feelings and combining colors, to establish the perception of safety within the mind and body. Recall our previous definition of hypnosis as a bypass of the critical faculty?

What makes these techniques different and more in depth then hypnosis is that rather than *bypassing* the critical faculty, we are going to use *all* parts of the mind including your critical faculty and the conscious mind.

The conscious mind will be utilized in these methods rather than bypassed, ignored and set aside which is what typically happens in meditation and hypnosis. Using all areas of the mind allows us to go deeper for more efficient and permanent results.

All areas of the mind model, including the critical faculty, responds to colors which communicate specific brain wave frequencies.

Colors, like frequencies, are of an infinite continuum. There are endless ranges of reds, greens and blues and whatever other color comes up in your awareness when asked, has nothing to do with that color but more to do with the *complex holographic data* and regions of information that you access by simply asking "What color comes to my mind?"

The colors you visualize when you are prompted to notice, are unique to your perception and vital to your own specific holographic nervous system. Note: there is no such thing as an incorrect answer when asking your mind what frequency. (by asking what color) It will always answer first, always answer correctly, you'll think you're making it up because it won't make logical sense and you may have an urge to edit it.

Go with your very first impression as that will be your correct answer.

Let's begin the process of anchoring ourselves into safety. First, find a location where you can sit comfortably with your back straight and feet flat on the ground and a place that you feel comfortable enough to settle in and relax. Ensure that you have prepared yourself by using the restroom if necessary or drinking a glass of water.

Once you have selected the location where you can sit comfortably and minimize interruptions, slowly close your eyes.

To begin giving our nervous system the signal of safety, start by observing your breath. Put all your attention on your breath coming in and going out. To the best of your ability slow your breathing down to a comfortable pace and begin to time your inhales, breathing through your nose, to a comfortable count of five. Slowly release your exhales to account of seven and repeat the process.

1. Breathe slowly in to the count of 5.
2. Exhale to the count of 7.
3. Repeat the process until you feel a relaxation.

Now I want you to imagine a location where you have visited before, and it gave you a *complete feeling of safety.*

It doesn't matter if it was 10 years ago, or it was something you recall from your childhood. It could have been at your grandmother's house when you were a child, a garden, or a beach you visited on vacation. It may have been a cabin in the mountains, or it could even be your current living room in your present home.

Sometimes, a person realizes that they have never felt safe before. In this case we will create one. It doesn't matter how strange it may seem. I have had people imagine a location that they did not visit in the past but to them it provided safety. One such case with a female patient who chose an imaginary concrete bunker underground completely hidden with three feet of concrete walls and only enough room for her!

One patient told me his safe place was another planet where he was the only occupant living on this planet. You get the idea. Take a moment and imagine of location of your choosing that would make you feel safe or a place you have visited before that gave you the feeling of safety.

Maintaining a slow steady breathing rate, I want you to go to that safe place in your mind. See everything you see there. Let it all come back to your visual awareness and crystal-clear high definition. *See it* just as clearly as the day you were there. Notice all the details.

Now I want you to *listen* to all the sounds that you hear at this safe place. Listen very carefully to all the noises in the background of this location.

Most importantly, *feel* those feelings that this safe place gives you. Remember how this location made you feel and allow those feelings just to ripple through your body like waves of water crossing a still calm pool.

Allow yourself to smell the smells that you recall at this location. Let those smells come fully in your awareness.

Notice any tastes that come into your awareness. Allow yourself to be absorbed in those tastes.

As you are there in your safe place, seeing what you see, hearing the sounds you hear, feeling these wonderful feelings that this place gives you and smelling those smells and tasting those tastes, I want you to notice there's a place in your body where you feel these feelings of safety emerging from. A place where you feel these feelings originating from and growing from in your body.

Remember *feel it* don't think it. First impression: where do you fill this location in your body? Allow your hand to move right to that location and point exactly where you feel it.

As you point to that location in your body, with your imagination, keeping your eyes closed, look with your intuitive mind at that location where you're pointing, and ask yourself "What color represents this safe feeling?" You'll suddenly notice a color (or several colors) that represents the vibrational data of information aligned with the feeling of safety as it comes into your awareness.

This color is analogous to the frequency of your safe location and because it is holographic in nature, the color alone contains enough of the waveform information saturated with all the attributes, characteristics, and traits of this safe place.

Said another way, ask yourself "What color represents this safe place?"

Consciously connect your breath with that safe color and breathe that into your body. <u>Breath is the link between the soul and the physical body</u> and by establishing this safe frequency, displayed as a color to the conscious mind, and breathing it into the body, you will give your entire subconscious mind the signal of safety.

Breathe that safe color all the way into your body observing it, visualizing it, allowing it to flow into you, into your lungs, into your heart, into your circulation, merging with every cell in your body. Imagine you are filling yourself up with this safe color similar to a glass or a bottle under a faucet.

Observe it with your imagination and allow that endless and limitless color to continue flowing in with every breath and allowing it to keep filling up your body. Notice how your body shifts and relaxes as you allow the color to fill you up.

*If you have trouble with visualizing a color, use a sound, a feeling, a smell or a taste that you identified in your safe place and let it resonate throughout your entire body.

After a moment, scan your body for any tightness or tension and breathe that color into that area and notice how it changes.

This is the first step before we begin the deeper techniques as this establishes safety into your subconscious mind. Many people find this very soothing and comforting and within moments your body and mind match the state of safety as if you were in that location. You can do this anytime and anyplace. We should always anchor ourselves into safety before we go into the deeper techniques.

1. Establish your safe place.
2. What color represents this safe place?
3. Breathe that color, sound, taste, smell into your entire body.

Beginning the Process of Clearing Up Our Vibrational Signal: Holographic Deletion

[Precautionary notice: if during any moments in this procedure you begin to feel overwhelmed or frightened by the intensity of the feelings, immediately return to that safe scene, and proceed only with the aid of a professional trained in this work. It is necessary for you to remain safe for this process to be completed. If you have an emotional outburst as the feelings come up, go back to your safe color and safe scene and proceed to contact one of our professionals to further guide you in resolving this.](37)

As you begin this process, you'll discover a lot of these things on your own but for the sake of doing this kind of work, I want to point something out.

One of the things you may notice is that when you try to revive a negative state, emotion, or a negative feeling, you'll tend to recruit it quickly, but you'll also hold yourself back from fully feeling it. This is inherent in our nervous system because as you begin to go into them deeply, there's a fear that you won't come back out of it. This is completely normal. *There is no emotional state that you can generate or recruit that you can't also pull yourself out of.* However, the belief that a state can overwhelm us, and as a byproduct of that we could perish, is innate within us. It is <u>not emotion</u> we will focus on; it is the <u>*body feelings*</u>, or somatic sensations, that are far more important. Everything in the human experience is governed by feelings. It is either a feeling we like and want more of it, or a feeling that we don't like and we want less of.

For this exercise, we will focus on the feelings that you do not like and want to get rid of.

Remember: the unpleasant feelings that you're carrying around do not mean you're broken.

Nobody reading this, regardless of your current circumstances, is broken. What the feelings do mean is that the systems that the universe put in place to protect you, to help you to survive situations, circumstances and events that you weren't equipped when you were conceived, during infancy or during childhood-- did their job.

They're holographic which means they're not just in the body, they're not just in the mind, they're not just in the energy field, they're everywhere and they're all connected and if you change one piece--everything will change. But if you clear a segment of it out and leave any segments remaining, if something triggers that, the feeling comes back. Take your time to clear each and every layer of these old feelings away.

Many people have experienced where they have worked with a therapist or body worker, and afterwards they feel like they got some good change work. That is until later, they run into a similar experience, and they suddenly feel the unpleasant feelings becoming re-triggered. Why? It means there were holographic fragments that didn't get cleared out.

Remember the law of compounding? If that feeling comes back and is weaker, it means that there are still roots active and, like a weed in a garden, the potential to regrow is certainly there.

This is usually because you utilized a change work system that targeted one aspect of the human being instead of integrating everything together simultaneously. This approach is different.

Each person has a Holographic Dashboard that encompasses the frontal plane of their body, and this dashboard is not only floating around the space around you, but it is also connected to the spaces *within* you. Remember, we are non-physical beings made of quantum particles.

The technique of Holographic Deletion is highly effective at clearing out the entire holographic imprints. It is very fast and efficient at clearing away unpleasant feelings from past experiences, including trauma, and it is especially efficient at clearing the ones that tend to return when other attempts have failed to provide complete relief.

How will you know if it worked? When you complete the steps, including interfacing (if necessary) try to retrieve the unpleasant feeling and notice what happens instead.

I cannot emphasis this enough: *If it does return, but is weaker, repeat it over and over again*.

You will start to notice that each feeling is linked to an entirely different image in your Holographic Dashboard. Each subconscious image, or construct is in a different location and will feel different each time you clear them. Just keep going.

Eventually, the unpleasant feeling will go away, and with it, all the stored holographic information in that memory container. You will feel lighter and deep sense of relief initially. With time and practice, you will recognize a difference in your nervous system as it will not startle so easily and the past things that seemed to trigger you will no longer do so.

Recall the process of bucket listing in earlier chapters? You must start with minor challenges *first* before beginning to throw larger, more chronic problems at it if you want to have success in clearing them.

Look at the list of **self-image constructs**:
You are not safe
You are too much of a burden
You'll never amount to anything
You're worthless
You're not smart enough

No matter how hard you try it's never good enough
You don't deserve to succeed
No one will ever love you
Money is hard to come by and hard to keep

(Feel free add more or to come up with your own list that trigger feelings that you wish to get rid of)

When you read these, you may notice a subtle uncomfortable body feeling. This is not meant to insult you in any way, but it is specifically designed to *trigger a holographic imprint* in your subconscious mind. This system has no ability to use words, so it uses sensations, or body feelings. This is how we know that there is a wound which still exist in our mind and body.

This list has been used in our Psychosomatic clinic (19)(36) for years because it uncovers something in the subconscious that the person may not be aware of. After all, it is the subconscious mind we are working with, and it does not usually respond in any kind of verbalization. In order to know if something is there, we must provoke it to see if there is a response.

After you clear the things on your bucket list, begin the process of clearing each and every one of those statements that you feel uncomfortable with. You want to repeat the process as long as it takes until each of these statements (or your own) has no feeling associated with it. Then you will know that the wound is completely healed. Some people have dropped feelings they have carried for twenty years in 2 minutes. Others may take a few days, or even a few weeks to a month to continue pruning away at all these old perceptions until the pain, the anxiety or the uneasy feelings that come up are completely gone. Then it is easier to focus on the positive aspects, remembering that your mind is the reality creator. Clear out the old garbage and focus on the new reality.

BEGIN WITH THE BUCKET LIST FIRST before you attempt at trying to clear this list!

The Law of Correspondence tells us that for every frequency, which is analogous to that body feeling, there's a sound, a direction, a color, a smell and a taste.

The entire system of Oriental Medicine is based off this premises. For every concept you can come up with you have a physical portion of your brain that mediates and modulates it. It's all simultaneous because the same parts of your brain that monitor physical warmth also monitor and control emotional warmth through a process known as *embodied cognition*.

The human brain is holographic in nature and at the same time, it's metaphorical, analogical and it's literal. Depending on your personality is how you are parsing that information and that determines how you'll focus on one of those areas over others.

The body feeling is the vibrational signature and the expression of a holographic information that has been recorded in your body; it's the node where all the different levels come together, and you can access all of it simultaneously. Following these directions, as well as being playful, pretending and being focused and absorbed in the process, allows this to become very user friendly very quickly.

It always *starts and ends with the feelings in your body*. Feelings, like ones that may have shown up when you read the list, are how we target disharmonic frequencies within our body.

These feeling states in your body are the navigation system that we use in this reality. Everything else, including our emotions we generate are just interpretation. Once we change the feelings, we change everything else behind it.

This is very important to understand; Everything human beings do including every behavior, is in response to a feeling that is in their body. It's either a feeling they want more of or a feeling they want less. These feelings always originate back to our template which is formed between conception and around age 5.

It either feels good or it feels bad. It's either familiar or it's unfamiliar and *here lies the obstacle for most*. Because if feeling bad is familiar guess what you're going to be drawn to? If you had a choice to follow a new direction that would improve your life, versus stay in the familiar, even if familiar means misery, guess what your subconscious mind will always be drawn to? Familiar.

Because that is what was there first. That is what *reality* is to your subconscious mind. Think back to the prisoners in the cave. Your subconscious mind wants you to be happy but if it must choose between keeping you "safe" by what is familiar and allowing you to be or experience happiness, guess what it will choose?

So, we have to go back, and we have to change those templates, imprints, those feelings because until we do, we are just pouring dirty water into a cup of clean water and hoping something better comes out.

This is how you begin to operate a practical understanding and apply this to reverse the symptoms of things such as anxiety or Post Traumatic Stress Disorder.

The vibrations in your torus field around you is a vibrational phenomenon and you have a range of vibrational frequencies. Each and every one of those is analogous to a feeling in your body with a color and/or a sound. (maybe even a smell or taste, depending on how your neurology recorded it) As you access the feelings, the colors and the sounds, or the correspondences, you tap into more aspects of the holographic data within the neurology, and you activate more power, depth and ultimately control and the more rapidly you can change it.

Although it may seem like an overwhelming experience that you have endured, understand that to your nervous system, it is *just recorded data*. Remember, one of the characteristics of your subconscious mind is that is organizes things, including all your past events, by what they have in common. Knowing this, makes sense that every trauma or overwhelming experience that you have had, which are of a similar resonance, are stored inside of that holographic container which is the exact location of the body feeling. If you feel it in more than one place, it means that there are fragments of it scattered throughout your body.

Once you understand there is a vibrational reality to these certain frequencies, are missing, we add those frequencies back to the system, the trauma goes away, because now the drop (pocket of consciousness) has merged back into the ocean (flow of consciousness), and you can heal.

Although you cannot change what happened in the past, as we don't yet have the means to use a time-machine, proper usage of this technique will completely de-potentiate the charge in your body that the experience created. It may take practice and getting used to but stay diligent and persistent and do it over and over. It will be one of the most helpful practices you could ever do!

For example, when I have a patient who comes to me because they are going through a divorce or a bad breakup and when I say, go back to the first scene situation or event that is the source of that feeling, you know where they end up going? Sometime in their life between ages zero to five, and this happens nine times out of ten times.

When we resolve the wound there, suddenly the new divorce or break up no longer bothers them at all. Although this method of regression to cause is beyond the scope of what this book covers, Holographic Deletion is a very fast and deep way to also neutralize a stored holographic imprint, which behaves like a persistent wound. I have used it with tremendous success on all kinds of emotional traumas, including my own!

Getting Started

In order to properly do a Holographic Deletion, it starts with finding a feeling in your body, a feeling that you have that you want to change. In your mind, rank the feeling on a 1 to 10 scale, with 10 being the most intense. (If you want to be successful with this, do not begin the process with any 8s or 9s or 10s until you bucket list properly!)

For this exercise, choose something that bothers you with the intensity of a 2 or 3 on your ranking scale.

Now, being focused and absorbed on that feeling with your mind, allow your hand, (which has tremendous neurological connection to the landscape of the brain, and it "knows" exactly where to go) to point at the feeling in your body. The key is to you *do not think* about it, but *to feel it* and allow it to happen. <u>Go with your very first impression</u>.

After you point at the location in your body, the next thing you do is pretend that there is an image, a picture, or a silhouette of something floating in the holographic field of your torus field in front you—a picture that you can reach out and touch with your other hand. (Remember the scenario where I had you imagine a red balloon and it immediately appeared in front of you? This is no different)

Imagine an image that represents the feeling and find the picture or image in front of you. Now, with both hands, pretending and being focused, reach out and trace the perimeter of that image and put an imaginary frame around it.

This simply allows your mind to further target this subconscious construct, like a sniper zeroing in his bullet onto a bull's eye of the target.

Once you have traced this image in front of you, ask yourself, "What color is this image?" or "What sounds are there?". <u>Go with your very first impression</u> and you will suddenly see a color and maybe hear a sound.

Remember: your subconscious mind answers first, answers correctly, you will think you're making it up as it won't make logical sense and you may have an urge to edit it. So, ask for a color (and/or sound) and notice how your mind gives you some data of the holographic construct. The color is analogous to specific frequencies that are encoded within the hologram.

Take both hands and grab the surrounding frame of it and **slowly**, like you are increasing the size of a picture or app on your iPhone, stretch open the image and notice *how the feeling in your body changes*.

Next, shrink it back down to its original size and notice how the feeling returns to it's original sensation. If you desire, repeat the process of shrinking it down and increasing its size while paying attention to the feeling in your body changing as you do it.

Next, using both hands still holding onto the outer perimeter frame of that image, shrink it down to the size of a quarter, which decreases the intensity of it and move it over your head and move it completely _behind you_ and imagine throwing it into a trash can, into a drawer, into the flames of a campfire or even in a toilet. (whatever comes natural for you)

As you move it from floating in in front of you with your hands to moving it behind you, notice how the feelings shift and change in your body as the holographic imprint is now, no longer in front of you.

Recheck the number you ranked it at (2 or a 3) and notice how it has changed. Has the body feeling changed? Has it completely dropped down to a zero? Notice how when you try to bring it back, it is either very difficult to bring it back or it comes back very faintly?

If you cannot bring back the feeling at all, the holographic imprint has been moved, "deleted" from your frontal plane which is the location of your holographic dashboard.

Note: You may have feelings come up, yawning or even a sweat suddenly. <u>Let this happen</u> as your neurology is resetting itself. If odd feelings come up, allow yourself to feel them as they are temporarily purging from the body. Do not manage them or try to repress or avoid them. You may want to write or journal anything that came up in your mind, any experiences or insights that appeared or emotions that arose. This will help in purging this out of your mind and body.

Reviewing the steps of Holographic Deletion:
1. Identify a topic or subject that bothers you. Rate the intensity on a zero to 10 scale.
2. Ask your mind for the location of the feeling in your physical body: "When I think of this where do I feel it in my body?"
3. Point at where you feel it.
4. Identify the image, picture, or construct (it may be unclear, but you will "know" the location in front of you and your hand will naturally go right to that location. Don't think about it (or you'll get it wrong) just feel it.

5. Reach out with your other hand (the one that's not pointing at the body location) and put your hand on that construct.
6. With both hands trace the edges or perimeter of that image. (notice how as you do that the details come into your awareness.)
7. Ask yourself, "What color or colors comes to mind with this image?"
8. Using both hands shrink the size of that image down to the size of small coin.
9. Continuing to hold on to it take it over your head and place it fully behind you. Throwing it into a fire, ocean, or volcano, whatever feels best to you.
10. Notice the changes in your body as you move that construct behind you. Reevaluate the number of intensities which you ranked it and repeat as necessary until it's completely gone.

*This process may take several times to completely clear it or it may clear instantly. Just keep repeating the process! Trust yourself and remember that this process is shifting your interpretation of reality. Sweating, crying, yawning or the need to move and shake your body may follow as your neurology updates itself. Let it all out and journal anything about this experience.

Remember your torus field contains your holographic dashboard and it behaves like a biological filing cabinet that stores and retrieves any information encoded into your subconscious mind.

When you ask for it, your mind retrieves it and displays it as an image in front of you. Any image or stored holographic data in your frontal field is interpreted by your neurology as an <u>open active file</u> taking up space and being very relevant to your subconscious mind. Whatever data is there, like the example of the red balloon, is interpreted as a solid object by your subconscious. The steps will be summarized and reviewed so take your time to repeat this process and clear any unpleasant images from your torus field.

Most people who are not aware of this naturally occurring phenomenon have accumulated a collection of life's experiences, such as a bankruptcy, a divorce, a loss of a loved one or pet, or other unpleasant exposures and their **holographic dashboard is saturated** with irksome, irritating, troublesome and displeasing past experiences.

Imagine for a moment you have a Feng shui professional come visit your home. If this person decided to hang a picture in your living room of the most horrible unpleasant image that you've ever seen, would you leave it there? Probably not! So, why would you keep one in front of you, displayed as an operating, unpleasant past experiences in your holographic dashboard?

Remember, these holographic constructs are very relevant to your neurology. To your subconscious mind they are there. They are operating, they're burning up resources, they are responsible for all forms of flashbacks, as every time you have a panic attack, an image in front of you, that is displayed within your holographic dashboard, has just triggered your subconscious mind's attention, but up until this point you didn't know how to operate the system.

All you need to do to change it is, point where you feel it in your body, reach out with your hand and find the image, identify the color of it, frame that image with both hands, shrink it down to the size of a coin and move it completely behind you. Repeat the process as many times as necessary until the feeling in your body is completely gone. To be clear, it may take a few times for it to go completely away, but it will.

I should point out that occasionally, a safety lesson is installed in these holographic imprints that needs to be dealt with. We will cover this in the upcoming paragraphs.

The process of isolating the body feeling, pointing where you feel it, finding the image in front of you that represents the feeling, reach out and tracing it (without touching it) with your hands and then retrieving the holographic data by asking for the color, the sound, perhaps even the smell or taste automatically gives you access to that subconscious file therefore, giving you leverage to change it. Then trace it with both hands, shrink it down, and move it completely behind you where *it turns that subconscious file off.*

That is how this process of Holographic Deletion works. Think of it as cleaning out the windshield in front of you where all this accumulated mass of data from overwhelming past experiences are still on your frontal plane, actively taking up space and staying relevant to your subconscious mind.

When it comes to human neurology and our holographic consciousness, it makes sense that every thought, feeling, belief, emotion and every daydream or every fantasy we will ever generate or can generate is built from the exact same vibrational data.

When a person has a PTSD or sudden onset of panic from a flash of a holographic imprint, it's built from the same system that we are working with when we image the red balloon.

The majority of the surface area of the brain that is devoted to each individual part of our nervous system, the two areas that take up the most bandwidth are the eyes and the hands.

Remember any image that you recall through your imagination, instantly is displayed in front of you to view with your visual cortex. It works this way for anything from a red balloon to your favorite animal, to the last meal you ate or your first home and the car that you drove to prom.

All these objects are represented by your subconscious mind as a solid object that has specific meaning. When you access the file and move that image from the front of you to behind you for all practical purposes you've turned that file off. Now it's no longer relevant to your subconscious mind and the *body feeling completely goes away*.

If it doesn't go away, we need to interface with it to address some form of safety lesson that your subconscious mind wants you to keep.

For example, if you go through the process of Holographic Deletion on something you rank as a more intense feeling, such as a 5 or 6 and the sensation drops down to a 2 and it just doesn't seem to reduce any further—no matter how many times you move it behind you, you need to further interact with this construct.

What you're running into is a safety mechanism that the neurology has put in place.

This comes from a specific part of your neurology that is designed to preserve lessons through various experiences. Through life experiences your subconscious mind has these learning moments such as *don't touch a hot stove* as a child.

Although you only have to do that once or twice and know, not only do you have the memory of a hot stove burning, but within the holographic imprint of that memory is an installed safety lesson installed.

These safety lessons are very common and must be properly addressed, through a process called **interfacing**, or using your hand to physically "write out" the lessons, experiences, and address whatever it is on the holographic image for the subconscious mind to allow you to clear that holographic imprint. (You do not need to know what it is you are "writing" — remember your conscious mind is the least informed part of you. It does NOT play a role in knowing any of this)

There are moments in your life when your subconscious mind creates a memory of an experience, and not only is it recording the images (visuals), but it is recording the auditory (sound) information, the kinesthetic (feelings), the gustatory (taste) and olfactory (smell) aside from the sensory information, but occasionally there is more to it than that.

It is also recording the story of what happened. From there it derives a meaning from the story. It derives certain lessons and those lessons become safety rules and as you start to go through the clearing process the subconscious mind doesn't have a direct path of knowing what to keep and what not to keep.

This creates a dilemma by which instead of deciding to just extract just one individual part, it keeps it all. The dilemma is that it won't let you get rid of the whole thing because it's afraid if you let everything go, you'll lose that lesson. You'll forget the importance behind what has occurred, and you may be likely to do that behavior or action again.

In other words, your subconscious mind does not trust you.

Interfacing is what is required when the subconscious mind realizes you need to be protected from it even more powerfully than just remembering what it felt like.

To paraphrase, it is as if the subconscious mind realizes that "I have to protect this person from this and so I'm going to make sure that he or she never forgets this…"

This is very common when a person has experienced heartbreak several times. The subconscious mind is the emotional mind and it's the protective mind. Without permission from the conscious mind, it will insert safety lessons in place in order to protect the person from potential painful experiences again.

In our example of a person who has experienced heartbreak numerous times the subconscious mind (to protect the person), build the perception that dating equals painful outcomes. It starts to assemble and recognize the pattern of being in a relationship as something associated with disastrous consequences.

As a result, a safety lesson is put in place and now anytime the person decides to go out on a date, the subconscious mind, to protect them, will seize any opportunity it can to keep that person from going on another date or beginning a relationship.

The subconscious mind is very opportunistic, and it will become magnetic for any obstacle necessary to achieve its goal. It's almost like an unknown, unseen saboteur is at work causing the boss to ask them to work late, the car to break down or even a bout with the flu when date night comes around. These are all attempts the subconscious mind, which is directly connected to the quantum universe, will do to protect the person without their awareness and without their permission.

It is so vital to get this, so let me explain the process of interfacing another way: Imagine that the holographic imprint you are attempting to clear is metaphorically similar to the English alphabet, complete with the letters A through Z. Now, you are attempting to clear this entire alphabet out of your nervous system using this technique, but the subconscious mind is wanting you to hold on to specific parts of this alphabet, as safety lessons or learning experiences, which we will say are the "vowels" of this alphabet.

Interfacing allows us to remove A, E, I, O & U (and sometimes Y), so that the subconscious mind will allow us to clear the remaining alphabet while keeping what it is we are meant to keep.

Now, let's say you "partially" interface without it being complete. In other words, you kept the A and the E, but left the remaining vowels in the alphabet and attempted to clear this. Since you did not keep all the vowels, the subconscious mind will view this clearing as a bigger threat (because you didn't keep the full safety lesson) then the imprint itself, and it will not allow you to clear the alphabet. In other words, the feeling you were trying to clear, either will not go away, or it keeps returning.

Take your time on interfacing (even if you must bawl your eyes out and write on the screen for 30 minutes or more!) to ensure that all safety mechanisms are extracted out of that subconscious program and it will be happy to release all the negative, undesirable, painful feelings permanently go away. Remember its job is to protect you.

Safety mechanisms show themselves when you are not entirely successful in getting rid of the body feeling after shrinking the holographic imprint down and moving it behind you. The body feeling remains or there may be a flash of memory that pops up, but the best way to know if interfacing is required is to ask yourself, "Is there something I need to keep from this?"

You'll immediately get an intuitive response if you are meant to keep something. You do not have to know *what* it is you're keeping. You Just will know that you need to keep *something*.

To interface, we simply add one step into the Holographic Deletion process.

1. Identify a topic or subject that bothers you. Rate the intensity on a zero to 10 scale.
2. Ask your mind for the location of the feeling in your physical body: "When I

think of this where do I feel it in my body?"

3. Point at where you feel it.

4. Identify the image, picture or construct (it may be unclear, but you will "know" the location in front of you and your hand will naturally go right to that location. Don't think about it (or you'll get it wrong) just feel it.

5. Reach out with your other hand(the one that's not pointing at the body location) and put your hand on that construct.

6. With both hands trace the edges or perimeter of that image. (notice how as you do that the details come into your awareness.)

7. Ask yourself, "what color or colors comes to mind with this image?"

8. After establishing a color(s), ask yourself, "Is there *something* I need to keep from this?" (Remember you do not have to know anything about what *it* is, just that you need to keep something from it.)

9. Pretending that your finger is a stylus, such as one on a tablet, place your finger on the image/construct floating in space and write out the "lessons" across that screen. *Everything that experience had to teach you will begin to show up as feelings, emotions and mental images or insights.* **You do not need to actually "write" anything; just**

scribbling or doodling and allowing your hand to take on a movement of its own is what is necessary. Movement of your finger (not actual written words) is the most important language of your subconscious mind, so just let your finger go without over analyzing it! Do not try to think about these "lessons" with your conscious awareness. It may feel like you are scribbling or writing gibberish, that is ok! Do it anyway. If uncomfortable feelings, emotions and even tears begin to flow from your eyes, let them! You are releasing repressed energy, and it needs to come out! Just keep writing so you can keep those important subconscious safety lessons and let the rest go. Some people have written lessons across the front of their field, without any idea of what they are actually "writing" for *45 minutes*, so take your time! If you do not remove all of the lessons, your subconscious mind will not let you clear this holographic construct, and the symptoms will remain.

10. When you feel as though the interfacing is complete, ask yourself, "Is this complete?" If you sense a "yes" as your first impression, proceed to step 11. If you sense a "no" as your first impression, keep writing! Go with how it *feels*, <u>not what you think!</u>

11. Using both hands shrink the size of that image down to the size of small coin.
12. Continuing to hold on to it take it over your head and place it fully behind you.
13. Notice the changes in your body as you move that construct behind you. Reevaluate the number of intensities which you ranked it and repeat as necessary until it's completely gone.

To be clear, it may take a few times until the feeling is completely gone, and that is what we care about. Because this data is both holographic and vibrational in nature, a person can store an infinite amount of data in the same location. So, don't get discouraged if it takes several attempts at clearing it for the body feeling to be completely cleared.

Some people may believe that they should do it all in one attempt otherwise it didn't work, and this is not accurate. The nervous system operates from the standpoint of repetition. Repetition, repetition, repetition... and then modifying.

Therefore, starting with the bucket list is important. The neurology wants to predict the future, based on past experiences, meeting what is actually there and instantly modify itself as necessary.

When the feeling is gone, the emotional charge is neutralized and the chance of it being triggered again by a similar environmental stimulus is mathematically zero.

Just to recap, when we point to area in our body where we feel the unpleasant feeling, we instantly access data interoceptively via our proprioceptive nervous system. Body feelings are how we target disharmonic frequencies stored in the mind and body.

Our hand is connected to the part of our brain that sense's objective information. To demonstrate this, image if you were blindfolded and instructed to put your hands into various buckets of water, each having temperatures from hot to ice cold. Without visually seeing any bucket, you would have no trouble distinguishing the temperature from the neural feedback your hands provide to your brain.

The body feeling is interpreted by another part of your brain that interprets subjective data, because nobody except you knows what that unpleasant feeling is like. This is due to every experience, including trauma, is relative to the *sensitivity* and the *perception* of that experience by the individual.

Pointing to the feeling in our body, recruits a tremendous amount of neurological engagement on that individual construct.

By reaching out and touching the image related to it, you access the corresponding information through your proprioceptive nervous system.

The act of using both hands simultaneously, the right and left hemispheres of your brain are fully engaged, especially when you use your fingers to outline the image. This entire process may be easy to overlook, or even discount, *but it works.*

It works by focusing and connecting all of the different divisions of the neurology, along with the surrounding torus field, towards a specific end result, using a coding system that all areas of the mind model understand. That is why this system provides very fast change.

Remember what you have read in previous chapters and how we are not physical solid objects as we may have once believed. As far as the neurology is concerned, we are just vibrational layers of varying densities.

Each of those vibrations is going to give a certain set of qualities. The proximity of the holographic image (you reach out and touched in front of you) to your spinal cord, determines the *intensity* of how your nervous system interprets it. The closer the image, the more intensely interpreted it is.

Once it is behind your spinal cord, which is where we move it when we are finished interfacing with it, it is now interpreted as over, resolved and for all practical purposes, no longer relevant to your subconscious mind.

If I were to ask you if you could imagine something that was once true (Such as you were once in grade school, or lived in a certain house growing up) and that memory you recall is presently no longer true and considered "complete" by your subconscious and you could point to it an image that represented this, where would you point?

Nine times out of ten you point to somewhere that is behind you. Why? Because this is the area that our neurology represents as being over and complete. Think how many times a person who is in a crisis nonchalantly say something along the lines of, "I have this huge problem (and they gesture with their hands to a certain location in their holographic dashboard, unknowingly and unconsciously of exactly what or why they did it) and I just wish I could get past this." Or "I wish I could put it behind me."

It's as if their subconscious mind is cueing them exactly *where* the "problem" is stored in their field and *how* to get rid of it, but they are not consciously aware of how to operate the holographic system that you now understand.

Holographic Reframing

For certain traumatic events, the process of deleting the subconscious construct, or the frozen holographic image in space that is crystalized into the mind and body, may not be enough.

Occasionally, more specific circumstances may require individual attention. We may need a more invasive technique, but we always start with the Holographic Deletion to keep any potential safety lessons by interfacing.

For the occasions when we delete it from our field, and write the lessons and for some reason, there is still a body feeling, we will use a more in-depth approach. This is where we will use **Holographic Reframing**.

To closely understand how this method works, lets briefly discuss the example the reason that noise canceling headphones work.
The reason they can cancel out background noises and various sounds is because of their ability to generate a frequency that's the exact opposite or antithesis of the ambient noise around in the surrounding environment. Within an instant, they play those opposite frequencies it in your ears and it neutralizes the noise. This process is referred to in physics as destructive interference. Refer to the Figure.

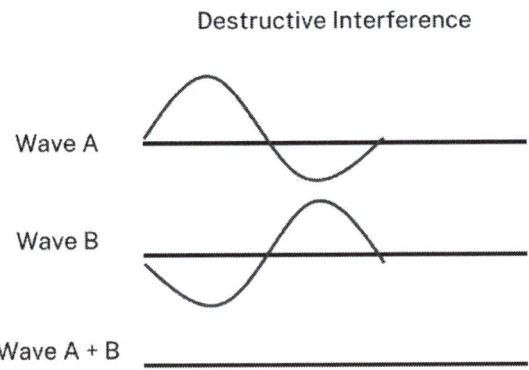

Destructive Interference

Wave A

Wave B

Wave A + B

Holographic Reframing works by the same principle. This technique is powerful and more extensive than the Holographic Deletion primarily because we are affecting the vibrational medium upon which all of that information is encoded in addition to the coding system itself.

Remember that our entire body is not solid, as the old Newtonian physics model implied us to believe with that false assumption. Once we understood that our bodies are in fact not solid then we can perceive these holographic distortions within our bodies and use destructive interference to cancel them out.

Remember how we start any of these clearing techniques. We locate the body feeling. The feelings you have in your body correspond to the frequencies that are within the encoded holographic imprint.

Feelings equal frequencies. To clear a *disharmonic frequency*, such as one with anxiety, all that is necessary is to focus your attention on the body feeling.

In order to generate the feeling that we desire, the *solution frequency*, that we can use to cancel out the undesired feeling, or *disharmonic frequency*, we need to use our Holographic Dashboard again to generate a "plastic movie" of what we would rather have instead.

We must create an imaginative movie in order to do that. It's really kind of interesting that we have a primary experience (such as a trauma), we generate a movie to go with the feeling and then we disperse it, modify it and unconsciously make all these alterations to it when it is stored in our field. The way we change the initial coding system to do the exact process.

We create a new movie that generates an alternative body feeling. *That body feeling is analogous to the frequency necessary to dissolve the original encoded imprint.*

Using our mind and our imagination, which is the domain of the subconscious mind, we can focus on what we want. Then from there, using our mind to tap into the quantum world of infinite possibility and create a new outcome of one which we desire instead.

Let's review what we covered in previous chapters. Studies and quantum research have discovered the building blocks of atoms which compose of everything in our known universe, exists simultaneously on an infinite number of possibilities and probabilities.

When an observer, in this case, you as the reader, focus your attention looking for a particular outcome in the field of energy, causes the collapsing of particles into a quantum event. What this means for this technique is that there are no limitations on what you ask for. *Everything is allowed.* This is where our healing from various symptoms originates from.

During my time in chiropractic school, we were told the power that makes the body is the power that heals the body. This is the very source of where all potentials exist. Whatever we give attention to originates into particles that become physical matter. When we no longer give attention to something, such as an unpleasant body feeling, those particles convert back into energetic waves. So, as you clear these negative unpleasant body feelings out, know that the mental body is to causative factor and wherever you put your attention is what your mind creates.

Remember these powerful words we already mentioned from Genevieve Behrend's book *Your Invisible Power* which accurately illustrates this behavior of the quantum universe:

"All space is filled with a creative power. This creative power is amenable to suggestion. It can only work by deductive methods."

In other words, all space including 99.999999999 percent of information within the atom purely works by suggestion and its entire nature is responsiveness.

Working by deductive methods means it works by both positive suggestions of life affirming thoughts, beliefs, and feelings and by negative suggestions such as self-mutilation or the ones listed in the previous chapter.

Before we get started, recall the way your subconscious mind (which is connected to the quantum world) will answer you: It always answers first, always answers correctly, you may think that you're making it up as it won't make any logical sense, you may have an urge to edit it and it won't necessarily be loud.

My mentor once said: The conscious mind screams and the subconscious mind whispers.

The steps for neutralizing those imprints and those encoded memories out of the body using Holographic Reframing are as follows: (It is best if you close your eyes)

1. Identify a topic or subject that you want to change
2. Isolate the undesired body feeling. Rate the intensity on a zero to 10 scale.
3. Point where you feel it.
4. Notice the location where you pointed with your inner eye of imagination and observe the location.
5. Notice how a color comes to your mind that represents the undesired feeling (problem frequency).
6. Ask yourself "What do I want instead?" (Everything is allowed-remember you are not working in a world of limitation; you are working with the immeasurable, inexhaustible quantum world so do not hesitate to ask for anything!)
7. Using your imagination, create a movie of exactly what you would rather have instead. (If you are not sure, ask yourself these questions: "What might that *look* like?" and "What might that *feel* like?" or "What might I want instead?" or "What might it be/feel like to be free from this _____?" This format of using the word *might* literally bridges your mind into the infinite possibilities and brings your answer right

to you within a fraction of a second. Create the most spectacular movie of what you would rather have instead, where everything is allowed, with no limitations, where you are the living your best life)

8. Watch the "movie" in full detail, crystal clear bright colors. Listen to the sounds in this movie. Most importantly _feel the feelings_ of what this feels like to live this life you are creating. (feelings are the solution frequency to the problem frequency, so do not hold back.) Smell the smells that you may smell, taste any tastes that are in this "movie" and give a moment of gratitude for being able to co-create an alternate reality. Gratitude is a powerful frequency, and this will help amplify the experience.

9. Once you have the "movie" exactly how you want it, perfect in every way, watch it play over and over again. Watch the details and vibrant colors grow each time you watch it play over and over again (using the Law of Compounding) and notice how it begins to take on a life of its own, playing over and over and over again. (You want to amplify this feeling as much as possible)

10. Ask yourself, "How does this new alternate reality (movie) _feel_? When you receive your answer of something along the lines of "Relief" or "Good" or even better, "Amazing" — ask yourself "Where is

it in your body that you feel this new feeling?"

11. Point to the area in your body where the new desired feeling (solution frequency) is located.

12. Observe the location with your inner eye of imagination and notice the color that comes to mind that represents the new feeling. (Use a smell, a sound, or a feeling as well if applicable)

13. Imagine the new color(s) (solution frequency) "breathing" or washing through the location in the body where the old color(s) (problem frequency) was imprinted. Imagine it as hot water washing over an ice cube (imagination helps) and notice how the older, previous color (undesired feeling) begins to dissipate, dissolve, or disappear as the new color (desired feeling) washes over it.

14. Keep breathing (or washing) the new color over it until it either completely disappears, or if something else occurs. Repeat as necessary. If you reach a point where you observe a change, yet there is a new color, shape, sound, smell, or taste emerges, and the solution frequency is no longer having an impact on clearing it, ask yourself "If my higher mind could send me a color, series of colors, a sound, smell, taste or a feeling to completely dissolve it,

what *might* that color, sound, etc., be?" As the new color comes into your mind, use it on the remaining problem frequency until it is gone. If the problem frequency color changes or "moves" to another location in the body, repeat the same process.

15. Repeat the process until the undesired body feeling(s) are completely gone. When you finish and notice that both the (problem frequency) feeling and the color are completely gone, attempt to bring back the unpleasant feeling. This is to ensure that all of the holographic fragments are completely neutralized, and the chance of a recurrent trigger is zeroed out. When you are complete, reevaluate the number of intensity that you rated it. When you reach a zero, the process is complete.

*You may find it very helpful to incorporate Holographic Deletion with this technique, interfacing, if necessary, to fully zero out the unpleasant feelings.

Don't underestimate the simplicity of this. It is experiences that made us who we are and made us ultimately feel the way we do. PTSD, for example is caused by an experience. To reinvent ourselves, we need to change the code of how our body interprets those experiences. If we need to change any part of ourselves, including our self-image, which is formed by experiences between ages zero to five, and those experiences are not available to us, we can make them synthetically using these proven methods and our subconscious mind and our neurology cannot tell the difference.

This is amongst the least invasive, least information dependent technique yet time and time again it has proven itself clinically on multiple occasions for reversing the effects of PTSD, panic attacks, anxiety, depression, and other undesired emotional states.

Conclusion and the Ongoing Process of Re-inventing our New Self Image.

The process of reinventing ourselves and becoming a happy relaxed person rather than the hypervigilant anxious one who does not trust the process of life takes time. Repeating these techniques over and over is essential for us to clear out the skewed looking glass of how we have learned to view our life with.

I wish I could say it would be a one-time procedure and that's all you would need to do but the truth is it takes time and relentless determination to make the kind of neurological and behavioral changes that match the ideal version of who we want to be.

 That being said, I have witnessed dozens of patients who have dropped subconscious misery that they have carried for twenty years in a matter of two minutes with these techniques. Others, it may take a bit longer.

As you learned about the endless, limitless possibilities that await us in this Cosmic Internet called the quantum field, let's briefly visit how we can continue to communicate with it and reaching our desires.

We live our lives based completely on what we believe about ourselves. These beliefs do not use a spoken language, such as the one you hear in your head. It speaks and entirely different language as sensations, by which we interpret as body feelings.

Using the holographic based models of change, you can begin the process of clearing out outdated subconscious programs the same way that if you were going to cultivate a garden, you would need to till the soil, remove the weeds and any obstacles preventing the healthy growth and proliferation of what you intend to grow in that garden.

Ask anyone who's ever grown a garden and they'll be sure to tell you the effort and focus and dedication it takes on preventing the takeover of critters and weeds as well as ensuring the proper growth of the intended flowers, fruits, vegetables or herbs. Reinventing yourself is no different.

Never forget that you are a powerful creator and that everything starts in the mind. Decide on who you want to be, how you want to be living three months, six months, nine months and a year from now and begin to envision being that person every day.

Put all the details of what it's like to live this way and only focus on ideas, thoughts, subjects that are taking you towards this direction. It will do no good for you to put your focus elsewhere.

Envisioning it in your Holographic Dashboard is one part of it, but this is what makes a dreamer, not a scientific thinker.

Feeling as though you are that person right now is what makes the quantum universe respond. Feeling as if you are already a happy, relaxed person as well as seeing it, is what distinguishes a scientific thinker from a mere day dreamer.

Live as if you are that person right now. Place great emphasis in continuously observing each thought.

If an icky feeling in the background of your body arises as you envision this ideal version of yourself, get rid of it immediately. Clear it using what you have just learned. Cast it aside and just repeat it until the feelings are gone.

The most powerful teaching, instructions and lessons that have survived for centuries, dated back to the time before the pyramids and is written in millions of books all say some version of the same thing: for changing who we are, and ultimately what we manifest in our lives, it has *nothing* to do with what we picture in our minds.

It has everything to do with how we feel in our bodies.

Just know that this person in which you envision *actually exists*. This is a scientific statement, not a philosophical one.

As you begin the process of clearing out old programs, encoded memories of overwhelm, you will feel lighter and lighter as the energy is released from your body. This allows you to have is the raw materials to create the version of you that you desire. Who do you want to be? What aspirations do you have in life? What urges do you feel to achieve?

I want to remind you that as a human being, you have been gifted with the ability to focus your awareness on anything of your choosing. Taking the time to develop and manage this gift is one of the most challenging yet rewarding endeavors that any person can do.

If you ever forget that your thoughts have real power, like most people falling back into the materialistic mechanical world, halting the process of clearing out old, outdated programs is all but inevitable. Remember the conflict and the false premise that has been conditioned into us that are true nature is limited to a physical being of material with the inability to be one with Divine.

I trust you now understand that it's our perception that limits us and our perceptions with focus, effort and determination that can change us.

Once our perception of how we view our self-changes, our entire world and all the experiences it has to offer us change as well.

Similar to how the observing effect works in quantum physics, by peering into the subatomic cloud looking for an electron and having it transform into physical matter, creating the best version of yourself healed, trusting the process of life is the same process on a greater sized scale.

The greatest change you can ever make to yourself is learning to trust life, understanding that the universe behaves like a mirror to the deepest feelings we carry, and therefore taking control of how we view ourselves, how we view others and how we view life and give the universal mind a better image, so it reflects back to us what we desire.

This is the Law of how our universe operates. Clear up the signal that you give off and watch your life start to change.

References

Chapter 1

1 Hay, L. L. (1988). *Heal your body*. Hay House.

Chapter 4

2. Maté, G., & Maté, D. (2023). *The myth of normal: Trauma, illness and healing in a toxic culture*. Pg. 25 Vintage Canada.

3. Maté, G., & Maté, D. (2023). *The myth of normal: Trauma, illness and healing in a toxic culture*. Pg. 27-28. Vintage Canada.

4. Talbot, M. (1991). *The holographic universe*. Grafton Books.

5. Roberts, A. L., Huang, T., Koenen, K. C., Kim, Y., Kubzansky, L. D., & Tworoger, S. S. (2019). Posttraumatic stress disorder is associated with increased risk of ovarian cancer: A prospective and retrospective longitudinal cohort study. *Cancer Research*, *79*(19), 5113–5120. https://doi.org/10.1158/0008-5472.can-19-1222

6. *Dr. Andrew Weil: These Alternative Health Treatments are BS*. YouTube. (2018, December 12). https://youtu.be/inrdwYv_BjE?si=fMGK3mke0rL7a9JB

Chapter 5

7. Press, A. (2015, January 14). *Heart transplant patient kills himself in same manner as donor*. Fox News. https://www.foxnews.com/story/heart-transplant-patient-kills-himself-in-same-manner-as-donor

8. Dias, B. G., & Ressler, K. J. (2013). Parental olfactory experience influences behavior and neural structure in

subsequent generations. *Nature Neuroscience, 17*(1), 89–96. https://doi.org/10.1038/nn.3594

9. Psychokinetic action of young chicks on the path of an ... (n.d.). https://www.scientificexploration.org/docs/9/jse_09_2_peoch.pdf

10. Lipton, B. H. (2016). *The biology of belief: Unleashing the power of Consciousness, matter & miracles.* Hay House, Inc.

11. (Gregg Braden/Wisdom Truths at a lecture in Florida August 2022) MCCLINTOCK, M. K. (1971). Menstrual synchrony and suppression. *Nature, 229*(5282), 244–245. https://doi.org/10.1038/229244a0

12. YouTube. (2022, January 18). *Why 80% of NFL players go bankrupt.* YouTube. https://www.youtube.com/watch?v=QXkGeObfdp8

13. Hay, L. L. (2012). *Heal your body: The mental causes for physical illness and the metaphysical way to overcome them.* Hay House.

14. Wikimedia Foundation. (2024, January 31). *Edward Bernays.* Wikipedia. https://en.wikipedia.org/wiki/Edward_Bernays

15. *Allegory of the cave.* (n.d.). Retrieved from https://mitphoto2016.files.wordpress.com/2018/04/the-cave.jpg?w=825&h=510&crop=1.

16. YouTube. (2022b, November 6). *Childhood trauma: Dr. Gabor Maté tells Dahlia why everything goes back to your childhood.* YouTube. https://www.youtube.com/watch?v=Z7vrINUpXRA

Chapter 6

17. *Medical error statistics [2020]: Deaths/year & malpractice rates.* My Medical Score. (2020, January 22). https://mymedicalscore.com/medical-error-statistics/

18. Felitti VJ. The Relation Between Adverse Childhood Experiences and Adult Health: Turning Gold into Lead. Perm J. 2002 Winter;6(1):44-47. doi: 10.7812/TPP/02.994. PMID: 30313011; PMCID: PMC6220625.

19. https://psychosomaticuniversity.com/

20. *Educo, Educas, educare A, Educavi, educatum verb.* educo, educas, educare A, educavi, educatum - Latin is Simple Online Dictionary. (n.d.-b). https://www.latin-is-simple.com/en/vocabulary/verb/242/

21. Wikimedia Foundation. (2024b, February 16). *René Descartes.* Wikipedia. https://en.wikipedia.org/wiki/Ren%C3%A9_Descartes

22. Sheldrake, R. (2020). *Science delusion.* HodderStoughton.

23. Journal of Consciousness Exploration & Research | August 2016 | Volume 7 | Issue 7 | pp. 524-543 Matloff, G. L., Can Panpsychism Become an Observational Science

24. Tompkins, P., & Bird, C. (1973a). *The secret life of plants.* Harper & Row.

25. YouTube. (2016, January 28). *Water memory (2014 documentary About nobel prize Laureate Luc Montagnier).* YouTube. https://www.youtube.com/watch?v=R8VyUsVOic0

26. McTaggart, L. (2008). *The field: The quest for the secret force of the universe.* Harper.

27. Peter D. Gluckmam and Mark A. Hanson, "Living with the Past: Evolution, Development, and Patterns of Disease," *Science* 305, no 5691 (September 17, 2004): 1733-36.

28. Shonkoff JP, Richter L, van der Gaag J, Bhutta ZA. An integrated scientific framework for child survival and early childhood development. Pediatrics. 2012 Feb;129(2):e460-72. doi: 10.1542/peds.2011-0366. Epub 2012 Jan 4. PMID: 22218840.

29. SCHWARZ BE. Ordeal by serpents, fire and strychnine. A study of some provocative psychosomatic phenomena. Psychiatr Q. 1960 Jul;34:405-29. doi: 10.1007/BF01562423. PMID: 13749151.

30. Schaefer, S. M., Morozink Boylan, J., van Reekum, C. M., Lapate, R. C., Norris, C. J., Ryff, C. D., & Davidson, R. J. (2013). Purpose in life predicts better emotional recovery from negative stimuli. *PLoS ONE*, *8*(11). https://doi.org/10.1371/journal.pone.0080329

Chapter 7

31. McCraty R, Atkinson M, Bradley RT. Electrophysiological evidence of intuition: part 1 The surprising role of the heart. J. Alternative and Complementary Medicine 2004; 10(1):138-43 [PubMed]

32. J.A. Armour, J.L. Ardell, Neurocardiology, Oxford University Press, 1994

33. YouTube. (2020a, March 11). *Rupert Sheldrake: The mind beyond the brain.* YouTube. https://www.youtube.com/watch?v=O-5gnp5l2kc

34. *Full CIA gateway document : United States Department of the army : Free download, borrow, and streaming.* Internet Archive. (1983, June 9).

https://archive.org/details/cia-
gateway/page/2/mode/2up

Chapter 8

35. Rosenthal, Robert, and Ralph L. Rosnow. 2008. Essentials of Behavioral Research: Methods and Data Analysis. Third Edition. New York: McGraw-Hill.

36. KD;, E. N. M. (n.d.). *Does rejection hurt? an FMRI study of Social Exclusion.* Science (New York, N.Y.). https://pubmed.ncbi.nlm.nih.gov/14551436/

37. Beebe, C. (1999b). *Molecules of emotion: Why you feel the way you feel.* Simon & Schuster.

38. For professional help contact https://thesubconscioushealer.com/

About the Author

Dr. Gabe Roberts is a pioneering chiropractor and psychosomatic physician who has dedicated his career to bridging the gap between physical health and emotional well-being. As the co-founder of Holographic Manipulation  Therapy®, he has revolutionized the approach to treating childhood trauma, offering a holistic method that addresses the root causes of pain and discomfort.

With over two decades of experience, Dr. Roberts has become a venerated leader and expert in the field of childhood trauma, advocating for treatments that integrate the body's physical and energetic systems. His work has not only transformed the lives of his patients but has also inspired a new generation of healthcare professionals to adopt a more comprehensive approach to healing.

Beyond his professional endeavours, Dr. Roberts is a prolific author, sharing his insights and methodologies through several acclaimed publications. His books serve as a resource for both practitioners and those seeking to understand the intricate connections between their physical and emotional states.

Outside of his professional life, Dr. Roberts is a devoted father, embodying the principles of patience, empathy, and unconditional support in his parenting. His personal experiences as a parent deeply inform his work, fueling his passion for helping children and families overcome trauma and lead fulfilling lives.

Dr. Gabe Roberts's commitment to healing, innovation, and family exemplifies his holistic approach to life and work, making him a respected figure in his field and an inspiration to many.

Don't forget your FREE bonus for purchasing this book.

FROM PAIN TO PURPOSE
COURSE
https://thesubconscioushealer.com/frompaintopurposebook

Would you like to go deeper in your healing?
For more information visit us at
https://thesubconscioushealer.com/

Additional Resources

WELCOME TO

Soul-Formation

TRANSFORMATIONAL GROUP CALLS

https://thesubconscioushealer.com/groups

CERTIFIED HMT THERAPIST

SIGN UP NOW

https://thesubconscioushealer.com/courses

Earn your degree in Psychosomatic Medicine.

Earn your Bachelors, Master, and PhD/Doctorate degree in the cutting-edge university!

https://psychosomaticuniversity.com

Made in the USA
Monee, IL
09 March 2024

54738517R00199